to try the mission. Therefore, I was ass cutting the rope away. This was a difficult task, because the rope was large, the water was dark and cold, and I had no diving equipment. I would dive under with a sharp knife, stay as long as my air would hold, cut as much rope as I could, and then resurface to breathe and catch air. Each time I resurfaced, I traded my knife for a newly sharpened one to help accomplish this exhausting task. This mission to cut the hawser loose took about 30 minutes that included many dives. Once free, the boat took off to our new location. After all of this, we did not use our equipment in Hollandia, but at the end of this assignment, it was all scrapped and was taken to the dump.

My tour in New Guinea lasted for one year. After this, we shipped off to the Philippines and served for another year. While there a tank landing ship (LST) came in, anchored and tried to leave, but could not. Its anchor was caught in a sunken ship's hold. They couldn't get loose so they slipped the chain and left the anchor. Later, I found out that my close friend, Sterling Chamberlain, from my hometown of Traverse City, Michigan was on that ship. On my way out of Batangas, Philippines, I spent time in the barracks waiting. There was a prison nearby. Our bad boys were in it. They had to have guards so the Provost Marshalls in charge gave me a shotgun and shells and assigned part of the fence for me to walk guard duty. One afternoon, a bunch of guys broke out of the barracks to fight, so I cocked the gun and yelled to break it up. I held my ground and told them to get back in the barracks. They did so, thank God.

Finally, I had enough points to come home. On my way home, I arrived in Chicago and I went to the USO for some dancing, as I loved to dance. There was a beautiful woman dressed all in white. I danced with her and when the dance was over, everybody standing around was laughing at me. It turned out that this lovely lady was wearing a white angora sweater, and it had left quite obvious white fur all over the front of my dress blue uniform. This lady and I brought enjoyment to the crowd around us.

All told, my tour of duty lasted 2 years, 7 months, 11 days. I was honorably discharged on February 16, 1946.

Figure 4. The USS *Copahee* (CVE-12), departing San Francisco for the pacific Theater. The escort aircraft carrier is shown passing under the Golden Gate Bridge on July 15, 1943. Navy Yard Mare Island Photo

BATTLE STATIONS, ABANDON SHIP

Walter Gallagher
US Naval Reserve, Monroe, Michigan

The year was 1942 and because of the severe shortage of trained Engineers and Deck Officers, the War changed practically overnight. I was a US Maritime Commissioned Cadet out of the New York area. We were on a training ship heading to all ports along the Atlantic Coast when the War started.

In Miami, we reduced the Engineering Cadets by almost 50 percent and then took the ship to a Tampa Bay location, where it had to be painted "War Gray". Once in port, I was told to take five other cadets with me and we would be met at the train station by an officer that would transport us to the Philadelphia Atlantic Refinery location. Two of us were taken into meetings and signed aboard the brand new SS *E.H. Blum*, a 12,000 ton tanker over 520' in length. Little did we know we would be ordered to take her to Australia to support the US Navy's 7th Fleet.

We had our "watches" assigned, and with only two days on board, not even enough time to learn every inch of our new ship or get to know our fellow crew members or officers, the unthinkable happened while we were heading towards the Chesapeake Bay. It was the night of the 18th. I was just coming off my watch and returned to my quarters. As I settled into my bunk there was an enormous explosion and I was thrown right out onto the floor. The noise was deafening, everyone yelling in confusion, and then the call to Battle Stations was given. The ship had been struck by a torpedo and immediately took on a list, SOS was sent out, and then the call to Abandon Ship!

We had to enter our life boats off the stern of the ship. As you can imagine, there was utter confusion and fear surrounding this situation. Once free of the ship, we could see that she had broken in half with the forward section and the stern sections forming a "V", and then the stern section sunk onto the bottom. The watertight bulkheads held in the bow section and it remained afloat long enough for the navy to eventually recover it. As luck would have it, our SOS was picked up by the US Coast Guard Cutter, the USS *Woodbury* (WSC-155), and boy were we grateful they came to our rescue.

It was a long trip as the USS *Woodbury* towed our life boats to the Naval Station at Virginia Beach. The rough North Atlantic waves were pounding, the boat rocking and rolling, and we took shelter under the canvas covering. We broke out the lifeboat's water rations and had plenty of hard tack to keep us going.

Once we reached the Naval Base at Virginia Beach, all crew were interrogated by Naval Intelligence and told we must never repeat one word of our experience to anyone. We were allowed to contact our families to let them know we were alive. Later, we heard that five

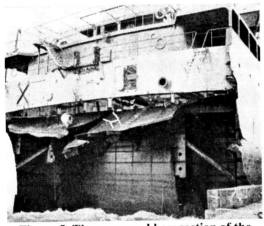

other merchant ships had been sunk the same night, either by torpedoes or by submarine-laid mines. Those ships were carrying men, women, and children; the loss of life was tragic.

The Navy was able to recover the sunken 300 foot stern section of the *Blum* and the ship was successfully rejoined in Norfolk and returned to service in August 1943.

Figure 5. The recovered bow section of the E. H. Blum, prior to repair in Norfolk, VA

Due to class scheduling, I could not return to my classes at the Academy until July 1st. I worked on the lake boat, the SS *William A. Irvin*, until the end of June. The *Irvin* was US Steel's flagship on the Great Lakes and she is now on display in Duluth, Minnesota. I was then able to return to my classes and assigned six months sea duty on a US Army Transport. We became involved in the invasion of North Africa. I graduated in December of 1943 and continued in the US Navy for the next five years.

A JOURNEY OF A LIFETIME
Betty Hale
Caledonia, Michigan

I grew up in Dutton, a small town south of Grand Rapids, Michigan. I went to a one room school through 8th grade. My husband, Carl, lived 6 miles away in the town of Caledonia. It was six miles away and where I attended high school. He told me many years later that when he first saw me come through the study hall door something told him, "She will be your wife." He thought that was strange, as he wasn't very interested in girls at the time. In our small high school, he was able to play on all the teams and was an outstanding athlete, which he would go on to make his career. He asked me for a date that fall and I turned him down. I was only thirteen and I knew my mother would never let me go with someone she never heard of. But when he asked me three years later, I didn't ask my mother, I told him I'd go. At first I wasn't very interested in going with him, but after getting to know him better, I found out he was so interesting, and had so much humor, I didn't want to go with anyone else. The next year, 1942, he went to Michigan State College, and I was a senior in high school.

His mother had two older sons and a husband in the Army. One of the ladies in the town worked on the draft board. Every time Carl's name came up she put it to the bottom, as she thought this one woman had enough loved ones in the service. One day this lady was sick, and Carl's number came up, so he was drafted. He quit school and came home.

Carl went to Camp Callan in San Diego, California, which was an anti-aircraft unit. The camp was on a bluff that overlooked the Pacific Ocean, a beautiful view. To a young man who never had seen the ocean, it was like paradise. They would run each morning through the shrub type, low growing Torrey Pines, which only grew in this place. We visited there in the 1980s and there was no sign of the camp, only a state park and golf course. The only familiar thing we saw was a street named Callan.

From there he went to Pasadena Junior College. He enjoyed it there though, seeing the Rose Parade and going to the Rose Bowl game that year. He and some of his buddies would hitch hike to the Hollywood Canteen where he would meet many of the stars. It was an exciting time for him. He attended a special program; I think to get into the Air Force. That program phased out, or at least he did, and they sent him to Camp Bowie, Texas. There they trained in the desert and he was with the 13th Field Artillery. He later became in charge of that gun.

On the home front, we had gas rationing, food stamps, and shoe stamps. When I married, I had to furnish the sugar to the bakery that made my wedding cake, as sugar was still rationed. My Grandmother gave me her shoe stamp so I could buy the shoes I wanted. We saved grease and tin foil. Living in the country, we grew a lot of our food and my mother canned it.

In the fall of 1944, Carl left the States for Oahu, Hawaii. One of his brothers was already there; so on Christmas they called their mother. He was stationed at Schofield Barracks. His letter to me was all cut up by the censor when he told me where he was, but his brother, being an officer, could tell his mother where they were. His mail wasn't censored. They lived in tents and every afternoon it rained, so there was a lot of mud. They continued to train there and were held there in preparation to invade Japan, where it was rumored there would be 90% casualties. Thankfully, the bomb was dropped and the war was over. There was great celebration on the island, with a victory parade. He continued to live there and was training the local Hawaiians. He was there 18 months when he had enough points to come home. He came back a Sergeant.

It was a happy day in February, 1946, when my boyfriend came home. I went with his parents to the train station. How wonderful it was to have my love home, and we could date again. We had been writing to each other every day. At the time, air mail was six cents. He planned to go back to Michigan State to further his education. I said, "You have been gone three years, and now you are going away another three years." Carl's sister picked out a ring for me and we became engaged. I said I'd work, and we decided to get married on August 24, 1946. That gave us time to go on a honeymoon and back to East Lansing when school started, which was the end of September at that time. His oldest brother was living with his wife in Arlington, Virginia. He was guarding the President of the United States and said they couldn't come to the wedding, but perhaps we could come out there and spend a week. My in-laws gave us airline tickets to fly out there. The tickets were $50.00 each round trip. I was so excited as we hadn't ever been on a plane before. His brother let us use his car, and we toured all the historical sights in the District of Columbia area. What a wonderful honeymoon it was. One evening, his brother took us to the White House, and we walked into the President's office and sat down at his desk. President Truman wasn't in Washington D.C. at the time.

My husband's grandmother had owned a duplex in East Lansing. She had died earlier, and his older sister, a brother, and he had lived there before he was drafted. When we were married, the downstairs apartment was rented, but the upstairs one was empty. We rented it for $65.00 a month. It was a furnished apartment with three bedrooms. We rented two of the bedrooms out to students for $6.00 a week. That bought our food. We used his $90.00 for rent. Our utilities were included. We bought nothing but food. I worked for Capital Business Service, an accounting office that kept books for small businesses. I was responsible for 45 accounts. I worked five months and then found out that I was pregnant. At first my boss, a woman, said I could still work because we were a "closed office" (her very words) and only women worked there. After tax time there was a downtime, I guess, and they let me go. She said, "You'd be quitting soon anyway." I guess that's what they thought in those days. I don't know if she had any children. Anyway, it was hard for us then. We had no car. One time I was so homesick and we decided to go home on the train. The fare was $2.00 per person, I think round trip. We took back milk bottles to get enough to go home. My husband got a job the next year on Saturdays. He went to school year around so that our $90.00 wouldn't stop.

Later, my husband got a job working with the athletes on the teams. He would pick up the shower and massage the players. There wasn't day care in those days, like there is now, and our mothers lived so far away. I stayed home with our son.

Because my husband went to school year around, he received his Bachelor of Arts Degree in Physical Education at Christmas. The next term, he was able to work on his Master's Degree. In the spring of 1949, he was hired as football and baseball coach and assistant to the basketball coach in Stanton, Michigan. These boys were all large, strong farm boys on the teams, and their football team won the District Tournament. One year the basketball team went to the State Semi-final Tournament.

We were there four years, and during that time two more sons were born. That year while we were in Stanton at the basketball state finals, we saw a friend who was the football coach in Greenville, Michigan. He told Carl of a job as assistant football coach in Tecumseh, Michigan. He was hired and we moved there.

We spent seventeen years in Tecumseh. We had built our dream house on the edge of town that had a creek running along the back edge of our property. Another son was born there. My husband wanted to move up north and have a small business. By this time, our eldest son Jerry, recently graduated from the Coast Guard Academy, was on the ice breaker USCGC *Mackinaw* (WLBB-30). He was married and moved to Cheboygan, Michigan. We visited them that Christmas and he told us of a small motel on Mullet Lake that was for sale. We stopped there on the way home to look at it. It had a new living quarters upstairs and the downstairs was much larger and unfinished. On Easter vacation we bought it. We ran the motel in summer and he taught math in Cheboygan during the school year. The view from our upstairs apartment was breathtaking. Mullet Lake is the third largest lake in Michigan, five miles wide and 13 miles long. The road to Cheboygan that my husband traveled to get to work each day was all along the water. People would bring up their big boats and stay a week and boat to Lake Michigan, or Lake Huron, through the Cheboygan River. Some people came along after nine years and wanted to buy it. So, we sold it and moved to Indian River, as Carl had one more year to teach before his retirement. I was glad to be free again.

In the spring of 1980, Carl retired from teaching in Michigan after 31 years. A colleague of his had suggested he apply to teach for the Army of Defense, as this friend did before he was married.

We had a letter stating we were to report to Stuttgart, Germany in late August. Our youngest son had met a young lady when he first went to Michigan State. They were married in her hometown in Florida in July 12, 1980. The young couple wanted a reception in Michigan so her friends from Michigan State and his friends from high school could come. They went on a week's honeymoon in Northern Michigan and then we had the reception at our home. The next day we started packing up our household goods; some to go to storage and some to take with us. A friend showed interest in buying our house if he could sell his. We left it with a real estate person to close for us if they wanted to buy while we were gone.

The post we were sent to was Patch Barracks in Stuttgart, Germany. It was the best place in Germany to be sent as it was NATO headquarters with a joint command of Army, Air Force and Navy people there, all officers that planned our defense, although at the time we weren't at war. The 1,000 student school was beautiful, it was built on a hillside with three floors and it even had a waterfall on the inside with small ducks on the water. The design won an award for the architect that planned it. My husband's room was on the bottom level corner having two walls of glass overlooking woods. There also was a new elementary building and after we left a new junior high was built. The teachers had to live off post as there wasn't enough living quarters for them to reside. We found a nice three bedroom apartment in a small town about five miles away. All of our expenses were paid except telephone and food. We were able to shop at the Post Exchange for all our needs. We had the same privileges as the military. The German people were so friendly to us, and I still correspond with some of them. After we left, we visited two more times. I guess we would still be going if my husband had lived.

Every time we had a holiday, we traveled somewhere. The first Labor Day weekend, a young couple who both taught math took us under their wing and drove us to Bavaria in Southern Germany. He could speak some German so they arranged for us to stay in a bed and breakfast. Also, they showed us how to order food in a restaurant. Thanksgiving time we spent in Tunisia, North Africa. That was like traveling back in time as in the Bible times, with children driving sheep down the road. They had a beautiful resort on the water, which was quite warm. We spent Christmas Eve in Bethlehem, Israel. We spent five days in Israel and five days in Egypt. That was such a dirty country, we all came home sick. Our tour was one of the first to Russia. Once we drove to Berlin, at a time when you had to go through territory run by the Soviets after WWII.

One Memorial Day, while living in Germany, we visited Normandy Beach with other Americans. After my husband's death, I wrote the following article about an amazing, random coincidence that happened to my husband during our visit to Normandy:

What's In a Name?
A Visit to Normandy Puts a Former Serviceman In Touch With His Namesake

My husband was born December 23, 1924, and was named Carl Quentin Hale. He never liked the name, mostly because he couldn't pronounce it when he was little. He grew up in the small Michigan town of Caledonia.

Some of the men of the village would see him on the street and say, "What's your name, little boy?"

"My name is Tarl Kitten Tale," he would say, and they would laugh. That happened quite often until, as he got older, he caught on to what was happening.

He was named Quentin for Quentin Roosevelt, son of President Theodore Roosevelt. During WWI, Quentin Roosevelt's plane had crashed and the Germans had put a fence around the site out of reverence for President Roosevelt. Carl's father's fighting outfit came upon the area and later wanted to name his son after the hero.

When Carl was in the Army in WWII, the fellows called him "CQ," which made him feel better about his name, as it could stand for "Charge of Quarters." When we were first married he asked me not to use the "Q" when using our name. I asked him, "What if someone insisted?" When he registered to vote, the lady asked him, "What's the 'Q' stand for? He said in his joking way, "Cute." When he got down the line we heard her say, "That doesn't start with Q."

A few years ago, we went to visit the Normandy Beaches and stood at The American Military Cemetery where 9,386 American soldiers killed in battle are buried, row on row of white crosses in symmetrical order. We walked through the area of crosses. My husband said he'd like to take a close-up of a cross. He knelt down on one knee to focus the camera. Chills ran up and down his spine and he was speechless for a few seconds as he looked through the lens and saw the name on the cross that read, "1 Lt. Quentin Roosevelt." He felt humbled, thrilled and proud to now carry the name of Quentin.

Figure 6. Carl Quentin Hale at the American Military Cemetery in Normandy, France.

Carl was always going to write down about his name, but he died before he did it. I, as his wife, wanted to tell the story of his name for him.

Ms. Betty Hale, Lake Ann

After being in Germany for 2 ½ years, we decided to go downhill skiing. There was a ski bus that left our post a couple weekends a month to various ski slopes. I spent most of my time on the beginning hills until the last year when I could ski the easier runs. We skied all of the famous named ski resorts in Europe.

We took tours to many countries. One Easter week we went to England, Scotland and Ireland. That was a tiring ten days. Before we came home we took another ten days to visit Sweden, Norway and Denmark. We were in Germany a total of five years, and we spent our summers in Lake Ann, Michigan. After we left Germany, we decided to travel to Mexico City, Mexico. While my husband was out in the boat fishing, something told him not to go to Mexico. He told me about it, but we wanted to go, so we did. My husband was employed by "The American School," a private school for Mexican students who wanted to go to college in the United States. Also, the children of the workers at our American Embassy attended this school. We had a nice three bedroom, two bath apartmcnt in the area where the tourists stayed. Transportation was so cheap; we could go by bus or subway and so we didn't need a car. The traffic was very bad there and the drivers did not drive safely.

After we were in Mexico for only about three weeks the 1985 earthquake hit, and 10,000 people were killed. That morning, my husband and some other teachers living in our building left for work in a van that picked them up. As the van traveled downtown, he saw many high rise buildings collapse. The windows popped out of some of the buildings like popcorn. I was still in bed but planned to go to a "newcomers" welcome at the American Church. My bed swung three feet to the right, and then swung back three feet to the left. The bathroom door banged open and then shut. The windows blew out, as one wall was all glass but the heavy draperies kept the glass from flying. The grocery store where we shopped collapsed. A fancy hotel at the end of our street fell on a parked tour bus. The American library was also destroyed along with the theater that showed English speaking films. The area was like a war zone. I ran out of the building onto the sidewalk, still in my nightgown since I figured it was an emergency. There were pieces of glass all over. Burglar alarms were ringing as the shaking caused them to go off. The van came back with the teachers thinking that there wouldn't be school; however, on that side of town everything was OK. My husband said, "This is why we weren't supposed to come here." We had no electricity that night, and as we ate our supper by candlelight, an aftershock occurred. The shaking was so intense it was hard to walk and keep your balance, as you didn't know which way you were going to be thrown. We lived on the third floor. The manager had put votive candles on the steps. I had to go down the stairs hanging on to the railing and groping hand over hand. When we got to the street, the pavement was waving like jelly. The traffic was bumper to bumper. It was suppertime, and the Red Cross came through with sandwiches. In fairness, we didn't take any as we had already eaten. The police said we couldn't stay in the street. We didn't want to stand on the sidewalk for fear the buildings would fall on us. We walked to a large, gravel parking lot. The Mexicans were already gathering with their bedding to spend the night. One lady motioned for us to lie down on her bed, which we did. I don't know where she slept. For four days, our family back in the states didn't know whether or not we were alive, as there was no communication. The first notice that our son got was from the military stating that all of Mexico City had been destroyed. We registered with the Embassy stating that we were OK. By calling a certain number in the states they could find out that we were all right. But for awhile the number was always busy. We went to church that Sunday and a ham operator offered to send messages to the states. The principal and his wife offered to let us stay with them. My husband was paid in pesos and the peso had fallen so much in value. When we tried to find another place to live, they wanted dollars. My husband's back was hurting him so that the doctor was talking back surgery. We decided to go home; if we had to spend dollars, we would do it at home.

We were home two months after the earthquake. We had built a chalet on Bellows Lake in Lake Ann, Michigan, on some property that Carl's folks bought when Carl was born in 1924. It is a great fishing lake. For the next three years, we went to Arizona and California for the winters. After that, we bought a house in New Port Richey, Florida. I went there for six years by myself, but I have now decided to sell our Florida home. During our life together, Carl and I traveled to all of the continental United States, Canada, Hawaii, and Alaska.

Carl and I celebrated 50 years of marriage at our church in Lake Ann. Our children gave us a gift of a weekend at the Grand Hotel on Mackinaw Island. We had the room named for Esther Williams and it was the weekend of the "Big Bands." It was a wonderful weekend. I said our 50th wedding anniversary meant more to me than our wedding, as I now had our family around us to help us celebrate. We had a wonderful, exciting life together for 54 years.

Our oldest son, Jerry, was in the Coast Guard for a full 28 years when he retired at the rank of Captain. He has a MS Degree in Finance from Connecticut University. He now works as an assistant to the President of a Boy's Military School and at a two year college at Valley Forge, Pennsylvania, two miles from his home. They have four children and five grandchildren.

Our second son, Richard, graduated from Michigan State University and received his doctorate from Ferris State at Big Rapids, and became an Optometrist in Munising, Michigan. He is now retired and they have one daughter.

Our third son, Jim, lives in Traverse City, Michigan. He is a graduate of Central Michigan University and the Great Lakes Maritime Academy here in Traverse City. He has worked for the last twenty years in maintenance at The Pathfinder School in Traverse City. He has two children.

Our fourth son, Jeffrey, graduated from Michigan State University and has a MA from Rutgers University in New Jersey as an Electrical Engineer. He has worked as a semiconductor design engineer for several corporations in Durham, North Carolina. He now manages development of advanced medical research instruments at the Duke Human Vaccine Institute. He and his wife have two girls.

FLYING IN THE SOUTH PACIFIC
John F. Huft
US Army Air Forces, Birmingham, Michigan

I started out by being drafted. I tried to sign up first to become a pilot in the Air Force – I passed all the tests but they found out I was color blind – my girlfriend Louise (who later became my wife) was with me and I was asked the color of her coat. I didn't answer correctly, so I wasn't accepted. After being drafted, I went down to Fort Custer in the wintertime, I think it was January of 1943, and I spent time shoveling the snow off the officer's ice skating rink. I eventually got out of Fort Custer and was sent down to Florida - St.

Petersburg. I don't know why I was there, but that's where I was. That was supposed to be, I guess, basic training – I don't remember now, it was a couple of years ago. From there I was sent out to Denver, Colorado, where I was assigned to Lowry Field. I was in automatic pilot and bomb site training and I eventually graduated from there, and ended up overseas in the South Pacific.

Figure 7. S/Sergeant John Huft of the 22nd Bomb Group

I landed on the south tip of New Guinea. From there I went to the east coast of New Guinea to an airbase called Nadzab. I was in the 5th Air Force, and on New Guinea I joined the 408th Bomb Squadron of the 22nd Bomb Group – The Red Raiders.

From New Guinea we went to Owi in the Schouten Islands, then to Biak Island, and then up to the Philippines - and ended up eventually in Okinawa. We were island-hopping as the war progressed.

On one of those islands – I forget which one – it might have been Okinawa, I knew that my cousin was flying as a navigator on B-24s. He was also in the 5th Air Force in another bomb group. I found out that his camp was on the other side of the air base, so I requisitioned a jeep and drove across the air base, found out where his tent was and went there hoping to see him. I found out from his tent mates that he had been reported missing a couple of days before. His plane was shot down while dropping bombs on New Guinea - he and his crew members bailed out over the wild part of the island. Some of the other planes saw them as they were floating in their parachutes and then saw the pursuing Japs picking them off - shooting them as they were floating down. While they knew the parachuting survivors were killed, they could not prove it, so they were declared as "missing in action" for quite a long time. I knew my cousin, Harry Stoll, very, very well. He taught me to play chess. He was a couple of years ahead of me and he helped me transition from grade school to high school; we both grew up in the Philadelphia area.

Figure 8. Bomb bursts from a B-24 formation. These photos taken during the attacks allowed for immediate battle damage assessments.

Early on I applied for and got to be a photographer and waist gunner on a B-24 bomber. I was in the tail-end of the ship. While we were flying to the target, we'd look out for Japanese pursuit fighters and shoot at them. If the Japanese planes shot at us we'd say we were "jumped." While we were over the target I took photos of the bomb drops and hits so the authorities could determine whether it was a successful bombing run and whether they had to go back and re-bomb the target. That's what I spent the rest of my time doing - flying on

B-24s as a gunner and a photographer. I enjoyed it. I might fly once a week or so, and the rest of the time I just goofed around. I got photography paper to print pictures on and the chemicals to develop the negatives from the photography technicians who developed and printed the bomb-hit pictures I took. I built a dark room out of bomb crates under the side flaps of our tent. I built a box with a light bulb inside and a Plexiglas top to print pictures. People from all over the area would get to know me and that I printed pictures, from the fighter pilots to everybody else. They would bring me film of the pictures they took with their personal cameras, and I would develop and print them and charge them for it. I made a lot of money doing that. I would get paid in Dutch gilders. Since I had a stack of them, I was called "Gildersleeves," who was a character on a radio show at that time.

I would fly on the bomb runs, sometimes near Manila on Manila Bay - Fort Stotsenburg, I think it was. Way back before we were there, the Japanese came and pushed the Americans, including MacArthur, from Manila onto Corregidor Island off Manila Bay, down towards the sea. And I would fly these missions – I have a list of them. We did missions up the coast of China and back - Formosa, Hong Kong, Canton, all up and down the China Coast, dropping bombs on these different Japanese occupied targets.

We were at the airbase north of Manila – Clark Field – and I got to know a young lady named Nottie Longsang. This other guy in my squadron and I would go to her house in a little village outside of Manila. Her family was very nice to us. We went to her brother's wedding which lasted a couple of days - there was a lot of eating and drinking and it was really quite an affair. We were treated almost like members of the family. We would go to dinner, sometimes on a Sunday, at Nottie's house. The food was really good – we had shrimp from Manila Bay the size of a small banana and it was just delicious. Nottie's aunt was a seamstress - she made an outfit out of red silk with pants and a kimono-type top that I took to Louise, whom I married shortly after returning from the war.

At one point while we were on the island of Luzon (where Manila is located) we heard that the Aussies, who were on the same

Figure 9. The front of an air-dropped psychological warfare card announcing "Peace in Europe" to the still fighting Japanese forces

island south of us, had beer. We got together some money and a couple of us went down to buy some. We brought it back - it was in bottles just like ginger ale bottles. We had three or four bottles - everybody was happy until we opened them and found out it was just water. So we had paid the Aussies for water. We weren't happy. Another time, we were on a mission, I think to Borneo or the Celebes or one of the Philippine south islands. We had trouble with one or two of the engines and were forced to land on an Aussie air strip for repairs. It was a Spitfire strip, which was a single-engine pursuit fighter much smaller than our B-24s. We followed one of them onto the air strip and I thought we were going to chew their tail off with our propellers – the Spitfire was forced to pull off the strip.

After we landed, I took my .45 and my knife that I had in a holster and wrapped my web belt around them and hid them in our ship 'cause I didn't want to just wear it around, I didn't think it was appropriate. When everything was ready for us to leave I got back on the ship and I couldn't find my gun and holster; I figured one of the Aussie's had found it and kept it. They were not very nice to us, maybe for good reason. When we took off on our B-24, most of the Aussie camp was there and our pilot, who must not have had very good relations with them, went up and circled around and the Aussies were there on the runway waving good bye to us. Our pilot dove right down and just skimmed over their heads, and they all fell to the ground and thumbed their noses at us. They were anti-American – their slogan was "the Yanks are over-sexed, over-paid, and over here." When the Yanks went to Australia on leave, the Aussie women seemed to like the Yanks better than their own guys – maybe we just seemed more exotic.

Figure 10. A B-24 gunner cleaning and maintaining the forward machine guns.

I ended up at a base in Okinawa; I was there when the war ended. Before the end, my squadron was ordered to go and drop bombs on Kure Naval Base on Hiroshima Bay on the southwest part of the main island of Japan. We were all lined up with our planes' engines going and the propellers turning - all ready to take off and drop bombs on Kure, and the word got around that it was really going to be something, because the base was really protected with Japanese anti-aircraft. We knew if we went over at 12,500 feet we'd be sitting ducks. We were all set to take off when we got word that the Navy was mad at us because it was their target. They pulled strings to have our mission cancelled so they could take over. We were kind of sad in a way, 'cause we were looking forward to the mission, but also happy in a way because we knew a lot of us would have been killed. We heard later that the Navy did a good job but their losses were more than 60 percent - and they were in dive-bombers, which were a lot faster than our B-24s. If they lost so many, we may have all been lost. Hearing that, we were all thankful that we didn't make that mission.

Figure 11. Officers and men of the 408th Bomb Squadron, somewhere in the Pacific. John Huft is standing third from left, wearing the cap, in the forward group. Photo, John Huft

After the war was over, I was still in Okinawa, far up north. I finished flying in July and was just waiting for my orders to go home, but I was still there when it ended. All those that had not finished their tour of duty had flown our ships home, so I, and a couple of other guys, who had finished their required missions, had to hitch-hike from Okinawa down to Manila. We just hopped from airdrome to airdrome and we finally ended in Manila. It took quite awhile - a few months because I think it was after Thanksgiving when I finally got back. We got on a Liberty Ship, the USS *Cape Canso* (AK-5037). When we finally reached the States we proceeded down the Columbia River and landed at a base on the Washington side of the river from Oregon. After only a couple of days, I got aboard a train that went all through the United States and eventually ended in Atlanta, where my parents lived and where I was discharged as a Staff Sergeant.

OFF TO WAR, A SEABEE IN THE PACIFIC

John Edmond Kelly
US Navy, Saginaw, Michigan

On April 1, 1944, I was inducted into the United States Navy, thrilled at the prospect of finally serving my country at this time of crisis; I looked forward to the experience with anticipation, excitement, and pride.

Upon my graduation from Saginaw High School, the Navy sent me to the Great Lakes Naval Training Center for "Navy Recruit Basic Training." This tough physical conditioning and skills training is difficult to complete even at best. However, we were not "at best." First, a third of the men in our company were ROTC dropouts who had received some previous military training in college, raising the expectations of our unit. Second, about ten percent of the company was composed of newly inducted men in their late 30s with children back home. Many of these men were neither capable nor motivated to keep up with the physical demands of Navy Boot Camp.

Figure 12. John E. Kelly, in his dress white US Navy uniform, with spats.

During the first two weeks of this ten week program, we only had dress white uniforms to wear. The traditional Navy dungarees and boots were not yet available to us. This meant that our early morning calisthenics and drills on the blacktop parade grounds were done in the white navy bell-bottom uniforms. Then these uniforms had to be scrubbed clean during the day for the evening physical fitness exercises, then again in the evenings to be ready for the next morning.

Somehow we did develop important military skills while being drilled into physical shape. Highlights included rifle and marksmanship training with the M-1 rifle, fire fighting and damage control drills in simulated ship compartments, hand-to-hand combat instructions, and swim training including jumping off of a high tower to simulate abandoning a sinking ship. These skills were to prepare us to handle real war experiences. In addition to the training and conditioning, our Drill Chief somehow instilled observable pride and determination into us as individuals, and as a Navy unit. Those lessons stayed with me for my entire service time, and in many ways remain part of my personality today.

The Pacific

After completing Boot Camp, I was transferred from Great Lakes Naval Base to Camp Parks, a naval base near Oakland, California. There I was assigned to the 38th Naval Construction Battalion (NCB), part of the Navy's "Seabees." Then the 38th NCB shipped out for Pearl Harbor on an over-crowded new Navy attack transport ship, the USS *Mifflin* (APA-207). The trip was quick, uneventful, and the food was pretty good.

Like most military service men, I knew that I would make it through the war alright. When I did get home safely, I thanked God, as I was very aware that not all came home. A review of some of the close experiences with death shows how exposed every military service man was during these difficult war years.

The 38th Naval Construction Battalion and I departed Pearl Harbor heading west for Tinian, a small island in the Marianas Chain, on December 11, 1944 on the tank landing ship, USS *LST-759*. On that same day, Admiral "Bull" Halsey and his entire Third Fleet departed their South Pacific anchorage at Ulithi Atoll heading north, prepared for heavy combat. Our modest convoy of several LSTs, cargo ships, and a few escort vessels slowly zigzagged westward across the Pacific at about 7 knots. Halsey's Third Fleet, with 12 aircraft carriers, 830 airplanes, 25 battleships and cruisers, 60 destroyers, and many other supporting vessels, moved swiftly at about 20 knots into positions to support MacArthur's upcoming invasion of the Philippines.

Figure 13. The Independence Class Aircraft Carrier USS Cowpens CVL-25, (The Mighty Moo) experiencing severe rolls in Typhoon Cobra's 100 knot winds, December 18, 1944. US Navy photograph in the public domain.

Also on December 11, 1944, unreported and unnoticed by either group, a tropical depression was forming southeast of the Hawaiian Islands. Over the next week, this "mild" depression drifted westward at 10 to 15 knots, passing just south of the Tinian convoy, as it built strength and violence and became Typhoon Cobra.

Typhoon Cobra challenged the Third Fleet on December 18, 1944 as a huge fully developed typhoon with winds above 120 knots. Because of radio use restrictions, encryption delays, and marginal forecasting information, Admiral Halsey and his ships were caught refueling the fleet at sea directly in the path of the storm and were unable to out maneuver the deadly storm.

"Halsey's Typhoon" wracked heavy damage on the ships of the fleet and sank three destroyers before the storm warning was sent out.

The typhoon lead to the deaths of 780 sailors. This total would have been higher if it were not for the efforts of the badly damaged destroyer Escort USS *Tabberer* (DE-418), to rescue almost 60 survivors from the sea.

As this violent encounter progressed north and west of Tinian, our small convoy proceeded west through heavy seas, violent winds, saturating rain, ocean spray, and pitching decks. We crossed the International Date Line on December 21, 1944. Then we pulled into the shelter of the Marshall Island anchorage to wait out the violent fringes of continuing tropical storms formed by Typhoon Cobra.

Tinian, Mariana Islands

Our convoy departed the Marshall Islands December 28, 1944 and arrived on Tinian January 3, 1945 under pleasant and sunny skies. We knew the weather had been bad, but did not know about our close encounter with the killer typhoon until long after the war was over.

While on Tinian, the older construction pros taught me to operate jackhammers, to drill and blast coral, drive trucks, maintain heavy equipment, guard our facilities, and wash clothes. I also worked on the construction of housing facilities, air base structures, a recreation center, and a hospital. The 38th NCB, along with several other Seabee Battalions, constructed the huge B-29 air base on Tinian. By mid-1945, Tinian hosted the two largest airfields in the world, with over 38 miles of B-29 capable runway.

Because of a minor hand injury, I was temporarily assigned to the security detail for guard duty. Some of my shipmates were guarding our dynamite dump at night. These guards shot and killed a Japanese sniper while he was attempting to blow the explosives with a hand grenade. The next night that dump was again attacked and exploded during the change of guard. Nine Seabees died; four off-going guards, four oncoming guards and the Master-at-Arms Chief. The explosion shook the entire Island and devastated everything in the area. Japanese snipers and sappers remained active on Tinian throughout the war.

When weapons were issued to me as part of the security detail, I received an M-1 carbine that had engraved on the gun barrel "Manufactured in Saginaw, Michigan," my hometown. Early in the war, my brother Donald had worked at that General Motors Gun Plant manufacturing these weapons. That rifle felt like a personal message from home.

As many other deployed units did, the 38th Seabee Battalion "sponsored" a special B-29. The adopted craft was the *Coral Queen* of the 398th Squadron, 504th Bomber Group. We painted a likeness of what we thought the *Coral Queen* should look like on the starboard nose of the airplane and a likeness of our Bugs Bunny battalion mascot on the other side.

All died too soon. The *Coral Queen* and her entire crew was lost on a February 15, 1945 Nagoya/Mitsubishi Engine Plant bomb raid. We learned later that they had completed their attack, but on their return they could not reach Tinian and had ditched north of that destination. Our Seabee sponsorship and airplane nose-art decorations did not bring the anticipated good luck to the crew of this particular proud aircraft. The 38th never again attempted to influence aviator's fate with our Battalion Symbol.

One additional memorable incident that happened while I served on Tinian was the visit by the heavy cruiser USS *Indianapolis* (CA-25), in late July of 1945. This massive fighting ship pulled into our tiny dock area under extreme and unusual security. We learned later that this ship had delivered parts of the two newly developed atomic bombs that were later exploded over the Japanese cities of Hiroshima and Nagasaki.

As a part of the unusual security drills, the Tinian shore based anti-aircraft gunners were conducting target practice. They were shooting at a target sleeve being towed by a smaller aircraft. After several unsuccessful passes, the gunners on the USS *Indianapolis* opened fire with just one huge coordinated blast that disintegrated the target sleeve, a dramatic demonstration of the capability and skill of the *Indianapolis* gun crews.

The USS *Indianapolis* departed our small Tinian harbor and headed into the Philippines Sea, via Guam, to join a Navy task force near Okinawa, the southernmost island of the Japan chain that had been successfully invaded in March of 1945 at great costs to the United States military services.

Three days after departing Tinian, the crew of the USS *Indianapolis* was tragically attacked by a single Japanese submarine. With multiple torpedo attacks, this huge and heavily armored fighting vessel sank so quickly that they did not get off a successful radio distress message. The Navy did not miss the ship and the crew of 1197 men until over three days later, when the remaining survivors were spotted in the ocean by a patrolling Navy PBY seaplane. During this delay the crew members were decimated by the cold water, exhaustion, and shark attacks in the open Pacific Ocean.

This sinking early on July 30, 1945 resulted in the largest United States loss of life at sea during World War II and occurred just sixteen days before the end of the war. Only 316 crew members survived that Pacific Ocean ordeal.

We were aware of the special B-29 bombers on Tinian, their special security perimeters, and even the special bomb-bay access pits prepared for these aircraft by the Seabees. We did not know of their special mission until the *Enola Gay* returned from their successful attack over Hiroshima.

Occupation of Japan

But the war did end. In the middle of the night August 14, 1945, the men on Tinian were advised that Japan had agreed to surrender. The celebration

Figure 14. Navy Seabee John E. Kelly wearing his Marine Greens, Nagasaki, Japan.

immediately began. No more B-29 crews would be lost. No invasion would be needed. Perhaps as many as one million American military causalities were avoided and many more Japanese army and civilian causalities would not occur.

At the time of the Japanese surrender, my unit, the 38th Naval Construction Battalion was training for the invasion. Our mission would be in southern Japan where we would improve, build and maintain a highway system. We would be the Transportation Battalion responsible for delivering the required supplies and ammunition to the fighting troops as they worked their way up the island of Kyushu.

The roads in that part of Japan were very old and narrow. The Japanese process of building their highways around and over the mountains made their roads inadequate and almost useless for our heavier equipment. The Seabees would have had to reconstruct the road system mile by mile as the invasion progressed.

The occupation of Japan began. I was transferred to the newly reinforced 31st Seabee Battalion that would participate in occupying the Japanese city of Nagasaki while attached to the Second Marine Division. Now wearing the Marine green uniforms, we loaded into Higgins boats for an invasion-like occupation of the Nagasaki atomic bomb devastated area where some 80,000 Japanese soldiers and civilians had died in the flash of the atomic bomb, and many more died from bomb radiation and injuries in the next few months.

During most of the next seven months, I was assigned to the newly reorganized Battalion Band. With no permanent work assignment, I and some other band members were assigned to day work details to supervise civilian Japanese working parties clearing and cleaning roads, ditches, and airstrips in the Nagasaki area.

When we first arrived in Nagasaki, we were assigned to a bombed out Japanese naval air base, where we lived for about a week in one of the open hangars with no privacy, heat, or proper sanitation. Then the Battalion was transferred to a former Military School facility in the small village of Omura, Japan, about seven miles from the atomic bomb hypocenter.

We, the men of the 31st Seabees, were exposed to residual radiation from the A-Bomb. Most of our daily work was performed in the area of devastation caused by the bomb's blast. Although the radiation risks were unknown to us, and to our Government, I and thousands of other US service men who served in this atomic bomb

Figure 15. SS3 John E. Kelly stationed with the 2nd Marines, standing at 'Ground Zero,' in the city of Nagasaki, Japan

destruction area were exposed to unanticipated and unknown levels of radiation contamination and many would be affected in the years to come.

Written assurances from the Army's Manhattan District Office, (managers of the "Manhattan Project" from its beginning) stated that "The 5th Amphibious Corps were verbally assured previous to 20 September, 1945 that the area devastated by the atomic bombs was safe for occupancy by troops." In December 29, 1945 they specifically confirmed that "both Nagasaki and Hiroshima were safe for occupancy by troops." With further assurances from the United States Navy Medical Offices in Tokyo and the Officers in Charge, we were confident that there was no risk of radiation exposure.

It turns out that there were discrepancies in the Government's initial assessments of the radiation risks. In calculating exposure they assumed that "The duration of assignment of any individual or any unit in the occupation forces was less than three months." The 31st Naval Construction Battalion unit was in Nagasaki for nine months until July 1, 1946, and I served in the Nagasaki area for seven of those months. While early records assessed that "the maximum possible dose any individual serviceman received…was less than one REM," the Defense Nuclear Agency (DNA) later assessed that "it appears that 99 percent of the personnel received doses of less than five REM."

These updated exposure calculations by the DNA meant that "Approximately 1700 personnel exceeded the current guidelines for…radiation exposure of 5.0 REM per year." Unfortunately, one key DNA assumption was that the occupation force's "mission did not include the cleanup of Hiroshima, Nagasaki, or any other area, nor the rebuilding of Japan [activities which could have dramatically increased exposure to the fall-out radiation]. These functions were carried out by the Japanese." As our Battalion Commander's monthly reports confirmed, we immediately employed thousands of Japanese workers as we built, repaired, and maintained the areas air strips and roads, an early aspect of our Japan reconstruction goals. The unstated operational element of that process was that every one of the 12 to 20-man Japanese working parties went out every day lead by at least one US Navy Seabee, and most weekdays, I served as one of those on-site working party leaders.

Coming Home

My service in Japan ended in late April when my "points" total qualified me for discharge. The schedules were set for departing Japan, and the lists were posted. Things did not work out as planned. When we arrived at the docks, we were loaded onto a LST for the long journey across the Pacific. The wartime LST Crew was reduced and now each Seabee had a bunk for the trip.

The trip turned out to be a fifty day cruise. Traveling in a large convoy of LSTs and LCMs the wartime maneuver of constantly changing course was replaced with stops whenever one of the boats broke down. When repairs could not be made immediately, the disabled vessel was taken under tow by a LST.

The food was pretty good and the weather was pleasant. For recreation we had basketball in the tank deck, evening movies, a large library of books and magazines. This ocean cruise eventually degenerated into a boring process of waiting for meals and bedtime.

We did stop for three days in Pearl Harbor. Those of us who found uniforms got to visit Honolulu for a few hours. Continuing the trip we arrived in San Francisco where the welcoming home consisted of a Coca Cola vending machine on the dock.

Again, things did not work out. The Navy Processing Center did not have any beds, so they issued us new dress blue uniforms and gave us a three-day pass. I immediately wired home for some cash. Several of us combined our funds and crowded into a waterfront motel for some sleep. The next morning after receiving the cash from home, I took my new dress blue uniform into a tailor shop so it could be tailored to fit properly, and my ribbons and rating badges could be properly attached.

All dressed up in our newly fitted uniforms, we returned to the Naval Processing Center, where we learned that we had been assigned to a military troop train leaving that evening for the long cross-country trip back to Great Lakes Naval Training Center.

When we arrived, we were immediately processed for discharge that day. I was Honorably Discharged on June 11, 1946, and returned to my parents' home in Saginaw.

Figure 16. John E. Kelly, MSC Graduation.

Within weeks of my return, I was enrolled at Michigan State College and using the GI Bill. My thoughtful older sister, Kathleen Carrie Kelly, had taken the liberty to apply, and had secured registration for me, at MSC before I even made it back to the states, and before I had discussed any college intentions with anyone, including myself. Before starting college, that same thoughtful older sister set me up on a blind date with her friend, Donna Ruth Hurry. Within four years, I married Donna, had our first child as my son Thomas was born during our last quarter living in East Lansing, and I received a Business Degree. In the late sixties, after an eighteen year career in labor management with Michigan Sugar Company, I moved into banking, serving as a Trust Officer. In the late seventies, I became a Senior Trust Officer and Vice President at Frankenmuth Bank and Trust, the position from which I retired in 1990.

After we had returned to our hometown of Saginaw, our two daughters, Nancy and Janice, were born. I was blessed to be married to Donna for over 53 wonderful years before she passed in 2002. She inspired me and made me a better person. Donna was an incredibly supportive wife and a steadfast mother to our children; her love for us knew no boundaries. She showed grace in strength and was the foundation that held up our family; leaving us with lessons that gave us the gift to be able to carry on without her physical presence. I now live in Traverse City, Michigan and remain very close to our children.

Not all came home. We owe those who sacrificed so much a debt of gratitude that can never be paid. These young warriors continue to live only through our memories, thoughts, and prayers. We feel pride for having served with them and some subtle guilt that they were the ones that had paid the highest price.

Long after we have all passed, the sacrifice of these men will be remembered by future generations of this appropriately grateful nation, the United States of America. **May they all rest in peace.**

★ ★ ★ ★ ★

Figure 17. Thank you note to John E. Kelly from Admiral Greg Shear, Chief of the Civil Engineering Corps. November 7, 2009

Figure 18. USS New Jersey, BB-62 firing from all three mounts simultaneously. US Navy photograph, in the public domain.

MY NAME IS NORMAN AINSWORTH KLINE AND THIS IS MY STORY

Norman Ainsworth Kline
Corry, Pennsylvania

In was born October 14, 1927 to Norman Jonathan Jasper Kline and Bessie Fern Ainsworth Kline in Corry, Pennsylvania. I was an only child who grew up attending a one room schoolhouse through eight grades and received a marvelous education. My dad was a construction supervisor in a number of war related projects. Mother was an elementary school teacher in Pennsylvania.

At about 14 years of age, all I had to think about was high school and girls. The next three years went by quickly with study, rationing and working. On Sunday December 7, 1941, as my folks and I were returning home from church, we got the news that the Japs had attacked Honolulu, bombed Pearl Harbor and destroyed numerous ships at our naval base. What next?

We heard a lot about the war from the radio and newspapers and were very worried. My family started a Victory Garden, planting corn and raising pigs and cows, so we had lots to eat. During that time, I completed high school and graduated in June of 1945. I wanted more than anything to become an army pilot. I turned 17 in October of 1944, passed all requirements and looked forward to becoming a pilot in the U.S. Army. I was Army bound when I heard of a similar Navy opportunity. I then launched an effort to go the Navy route. I was tested and had my physical at the Philadelphia Navy Yard. I went from Corry to Philadelphia by train; what an experience that was. I didn't realize that I was still a child, but my mom did!

I passed everything, including the Annapolis exam and got a Congressional Appointment to go to the Naval Academy but couldn't go because by that time I was already in the Navy. After a tearful goodbye to my mom, I entered the Navy on July 3, 1945. I took the train to Davenport, Iowa, and was classified V-5 (Navy Air Cadet Pilot Training) but was assigned to a V-12 unit (Naval Officers

Figure 19. Officer Candidate Norman Kline.

Training). Half-way through my second semester, the war ended, August 14, 1945. What a joyous day!

A comical story that happened on that day: There were about 100 plus "swabbies" on the street. My buddy, Johnnie Law, a green 17 year old and one of the swabbies, had both ankles bandaged up to his knees. An anxious news reporter was there and said, "Here is a wounded sailor returning form the war, I'll try to get an interview. What happened to you son, how were you wounded?" He replied, "No sir, I've got athletes foot."

After that, our unit was reassigned to Colorado College, another wonderful experience. I met Russ Leonard from Culver, Indiana and we became great friends. After we had finished our third and fourth semesters and were on our way to "pre-flight," things started looking bleak for pilots training; so after a few months, we opted out. We then had to finish basic training, "boots," at Great Lakes Training Center north of Chicago. Another experience, from there I went to Patuxent River, Maryland Naval Air Test Center for eight more months; very interesting! At that time, they had most of the Allied, Japanese and German airplanes, including the real "biggies." I worked for Marine Colonel Marion F. Carl, a Flying Ace pilot, and the first to break the sound barrier in level flight. At that time, I was offered a discharge from Lido Beach, Long Island; continued Navy life not appearing horribly exciting, I took it!

The next month, I enrolled in Gannon College in Erie, Pennsylvania and finished my junior year. Then I proceeded to the University of Detroit to pursue my Architectural Degree which I attained in 1952. In the meantime, I had met pretty Evelyn Harris, fallen in love, married her, and finished college. I attained my registration as an Architect in 1955. I eagerly pursued the adventures of a beginning architect.

In the midst of my pursuit of my formal education my life was enhanced with a growing family. It was in 1948 when I married Evelyn. We had four sons: Norman Dennis in 1949, now an Artist and Chef; Steven Jeffrey in 1952, now a Sculptor; Randall Harris in 1955, now a Contract Painter and Woodworker; and Jonathan Ainsworth in 1960, now a Teacher, with a Degree in Performance Arts. All of our sons have College Degrees including two Master's Degrees. We are very proud of our sons.

In 1957, I started working for Alden B. Dow, Architect in Midland, Michigan. I continued this association for nine years; what a great learning experience. I also worked for four years in Petoskey, Michigan. After these opportunities, filled with valuable on the job experience, I formed my own firm GBK, Greilick, Bell, Kline and Brown, with Bill Greilick, Bob Bell, and engineer George Brown which was really a good team; working there for 45 years and I loved it. I retired in 1993 and lived on the Old Mission Peninsula. We traveled extensively from 1992 to 2005 and enjoyed our lives. We loved it! That is my story...so far!

Figure 20. Beachhead at D-Day landing. US Army photo, in the public domain.

WARTIME ROMANCE MAKES BIG NEWS
Mary Lindley
Menominee, Michigan

This is the World War II love story of Barbara Reeve of London, England and United States Army Sergeant George R. Nason, a brother to Mary Lindley of the Village at Bay Ridge, Traverse City, Michigan. My brother, United States Army Sergeant George R. Nason was born in Menominee, Michigan in 1914. He served in the famed Company B of the 7th Engineer Battalion. George participated in the D-Day Invasion of France. In Luxembourg he was wounded in the back by a German machine gun and was paralyzed. He recovered in an English hospital for several months and he then returned to the United States. My brother's love story, one that came out of this war follows. I tell the story of a wounded man, blessed in the midst of tragedy. The prose of the time will tell this tale, as those words seem most appropriate in painting the picture of the actual events of the time.

I begin with the words of George in a letter written to me, telling of hard times, low wages, and even lost loves, which later turn out to be the way it should be. As you finish my account, you will understand what I mean. The correspondence reads as follows:

Co. B. 7th Eng. B, Fort Custer, March 17th, 1941

Dear Sis:

Well I think I finally found time to draft you a line. I hope you are getting along OK but didn't like the idea of your gaining weight. I've gained a little weight but I don't think it's possible to hold it. I'm working harder than I've ever worked in my life, but I don't mind, I can take it. We have built three bridges since I've been here on the engineering, two across the Kalamazoo River and one across two large hills. If you read the Detroit Free Press you probably saw them. I am in the harder fighting and working division in the army. In case of war, there will be thirty engineers to two thousand infantry men or artillery men. We show and help them to build road tanks and troop blockades. We build pontoon bridges for the troops, trucks and tanks.

We handle dynamite hand grenades, build them barbed wire entanglements, and cut and damage the enemies. Oh, I could write for another hour and I wouldn't be able to tell you all of my duties. But, I am going to get all I can out of this year's training. And, I only hope it isn't any more than a year.

Figure 21. Medals, ribbons, and devices of Army Sergeant George R. Nason

I've met some swell fellows here, there's never a dull moment. One thing that makes it bad though is the money problems. We get $21.00 a month. It's compulsory to pay $2.00 a month for our laundry, about $1.50 for dry cleaning, $0.35 cents for Veterans of Foreign Wars, and I get another insurance policy of $1,500.00 that's another $1.50. That leaves $16.00 and we have to buy cigarettes, soap, razor blades and other necessities. Oh yes, Mary, if anything should ever happen to me, I've got two insurance policies; one for $1,000.00 and one for $1,500.00 and they're both made out to Ma, don't tell her but just remember. I had $2,000.00 more when I worked at Fischer Body but I had to drop it when I left.

I heard from Ma and Johnnie last week. John has been drafted and Clarence's wife had a baby.

Will have to close with love, Sis. Just George

P. S. Keep this news to yourself please. Excuse writing.

After writing that letter, I doubt that he expected to experience what he did during the war. The following are two renditions of the events of his wedding. After all the tragedy, the silver lining and happy ending was revealed. Please enjoy his story.

The story of their war romance was summarized by reporter Fannie Hurst of the *American Weekly* in 1946 and printed as follows in the October 27, 1946 issue. That story is followed by a news report of the wedding, published locally and written by Berenice D. Murphy

True Blue Love Story

Gangway for a love story! It is a clear white diamond of a love story, studded into the mud of battle. Its very simplicity is part of its clear beauty, just as the white diamond, packed with fires, is rock of the earth.

The girl in this gleaming story, Barbara Reeve, apparently decided with wisdom well beyond her 24 years, that the basic elements of the good life are elemental. She has her own way of putting it: "I love Sergeant George Nason, because he is generous and kind and has a fine sense of right. What has happened has not changed those qualities."

What has happened to George is the loss of the use of his legs. "You don't love a man for his ability to walk," says Barbara.

It happened during the invasion of Luxembourg, in the battle to cross the Saar River. It happened to Sergeant Nason, while he was in the very midst of his romance with the English girl, whom he had met in a restaurant at a London railway station, in the spring of 1943.

Precarious days those were; loaded with hazards, blood, sweat and worse. Luxembourg and the battle to cross the Saar were already on the crimson horizon, but Sergeant Nason did not know it and Barbara did not know it.

So, boy meets girl in the murk of a London railway station. A young sergeant from Menominee, Michigan, where they do not raise their boys to be soldiers, on leave with a 48-hour pass in his uniform pocket, hoists himself before a lunch counter, orders a sandwich, turns for a look at the person beside him, and here, according to the sergeant himself, is what happened:

"I looked into the bluest eyes I had ever seen. I smiled at her and she smiled back. Then I got hold of myself and said, 'Hello." And she said 'Hello.'"

So, boy meets girl. As simply as if could have happened in the sergeant's own Menominee, or as simply as it could, or doubtless does and will, happen in communities along the Danube, Wabash or Volga.

Sergeant Nason looked into the bluest eyes he had ever seen, and before he left that café he knew what to do with his furlough! Forty-eight hours later, into which he packed a lifetime, he and a blond girl, Barbara Reeve, were engaged.

Just another war romance built on precarious sands of uncertainty, its horizons blood red, its hazards high, but an office girl went back to her routine with the meaning of her life changed, and a sergeant from Menominee left for the wars, with a higher love-of-life burning in him than he had ever dreamed possible.

The Army said the earliest they could be married was June 1944. But with their subsequent meetings, and their subsequent letters, given over to planning their wedding; their ultimate home in America; their future, together – what was a twelvemonth, after all; Three hundred and sixty five days of planning the good life.

Lucky though the good sergeant was in the fiery hell of the Normandy landing; lucky though he was, clear across precarious France, a German sniper got him in Luxembourg.

After that, Barbara did not see her sergeant until she was called to the hospital in Hereford. The facts were stark. The man at whose side she had planned to walk down a church aisle to her marriage vows was paralyzed from the hips down and might not recover the use of his legs.

It had all happened as suddenly as the miracle that day at the London lunch counter, when a young sergeant had looked into the bluest eyes he had ever seen. Only this time, the event was stuff of which tragedy is made. At least if you let it be. Barbara Reeve didn't.

Young fellows from our American towns have an inbred decency, a sort of chivalry, which they manage to conceal beneath idioms such as: "Cut the sob stuff."

So true to type, our American sergeant said something like: "The marriage is off, Honey. Goodbye. I'm no good match for the girl with the bluest eyes in the world."

"Are you going to marry someone else?" asked Barbara with what must have been ice in her voice.

"No," he said, speaking volumes of heartache as if he were reciting.

"Then you have to marry me," pronounces Barbara, just as matter of factly. "If you don't, it will mean that you and I will be alone all through our lives. I'll never marry another."

It is sporting to ring down the curtain on the remainder of scenes such as this.

The scene shifts. Sergeant Nason is back in the United States, hospitalized "indefinitely." This time the girl in the case accepts the decision, but with her kind of logic. "I don't believe he will ever walk again. But what of it? Walking doesn't have anything to do with loving a man. You love him because – well, because he's a certain kind of person. George is my kind."

One day the Red Cross drives Sergeant Nason, without explanation, to a certain airport. The London plane zooms in. The first passenger to alight is the girl with the bluest eyes he had ever seen and they were married.

It was not the ceremony they planned. As marriages go, it was in a class by itself. It took place in the Army's Vaughn General Hospital, near Chicago. Instead of a simple wedding, there was a motion picture equipment van outside the hospital, and cameramen, reporters, Red Cross workers, hospital personnel and patients were in attendance.

Sergeant Nason was rolled down the aisle in his wheelchair, through a corridor of more wheelchairs occupied by his fellow patients in the paraplegic ward.

Beside him walked the girl with the truest eyes in the world.

And so they were married – Miss Barbara Reeve of London, and Sgt. George Nason, Menominee Michigan, in a hospital.

By Berenice D. Murphy

At a full military wedding in the chapel of Vaughn General hospital, Hines, Ill., Wednesday, Sergeant George Nason, Jr., wounded Army veteran married English-born Miss Barbara Reeve, climaxing a romance which began in 1943 when the young people first met in a London railroad station. Nason is a son of Mr. and Mrs. George Nason, 309 Lloyd Avenue.

Spring flowers banked the altar of the chapel and the flickering light of white tapers cast a soft glow on the blonde bride, wearing a blue wedding dress, and the proud, smiling bridegroom, who sat in a wheelchair at her side.

The ceremony was as at 2:30 pm. A hushed silence settled over the crowded chapel as a Red Cross hospital staff worker played Lohengrin's "Bridal Chorus" and the bride escorted by Captain Madison Thomas of Battle Creek. Nason's personal physician walked slowly up the aisle. As the music began, the bridegroom, in a custom-built chromium wheel chair made for him by the Lloyd Manufacturing Company plant here and presented by a Lloyd representative and the Menominee Red Cross chapter, was wheeled to the chancel rail along with his best man, Clyde Lucas of Detroit, Army Technician, third grade, who is also a wheelchair patient.

Chaplain Reads Rite

As the bride knelt alongside the wheelchair, a soprano in the choir loft sang "O Promise Me."

Miss Reeve stood when the music ended and then the Rev. J. Vander Graff of Maywood, Protestant chaplain at the hospital, took up the wedding rings from the altar and began the service.

"These two rings," he said, "I have taken from the foot of the crucifix. They have been touched to the cross." He spoke of the cross the bride and the bridegroom would have to carry through their lives, and of how heavy it would seem, sometimes. And he spoke of the faith and the love they bore each other, faith and love as endless as the golden circles with which they were about to plight their troth, circles which had no beginning and no end. After the young people repeated the vows read to them by the chaplain the soprano in the choir loft sang "The Lord's Prayer."

The bride's blue dress, which she obtained by saving ration coupons prior to June 1944 when she first planned to wear it, was a street length model, simply styled with matching sequin trim and bracelet length sleeves. It matched her blue eyes and complemented her attractive blonde hair where the same material trimmed the delicate blue veiling. At her left shoulder was a cluster of white orchids.

The bridegroom wore the full dress uniform of an Army sergeant.

Reception in Ward

Watching the service from one of the front seats was the bridegroom's mother, who sat with her son and daughter-in-law, Mr. and Mrs. John Nason of this city. Across the aisle were nearly 40 wheelchairs, each bearing a paralyzed, wounded veteran from the bridegroom's ward, and each attended by a staff nurse or hospital technician.

As the ceremony ended the organ began the "Wedding March" from Mendelssohn's "Mid Summer Night's Dream" and the smiling young couple left the chapel, the bride guiding her husband's wheelchair.

A reception followed in the hospital ward. There a long table had been arranged with bowls of flowers and candles and in the center were the bride and bridegroom's tiered cakes, both elaborately decorated. The young people cut their cakes with a large knife resembling an Army saber with white ribbons tied to its handle.

At 5:30 pm., Sergeant Nason and his bride left the hospital for the Edgewater Beach hotel in Chicago where they are to occupy the bridal suite for three days as guests of the management. There they will place a long-distance call to the bride's family in England, the call to be a wedding gift to the couple from the General Motors Company, by whom Nason was employed at Lansing, Michigan before entering the Army.

Wounded by Machine Gun

Red Cross workers at the hospital reported offers of several small apartments near the hospital for the bride.

Gifts, including checks, and telegrams and other messages of congratulations have been arriving at the hospital since the wedding plans were announced Monday. Among the gifts was a box from an unidentified giver, containing three pair of nylon hose for the bride.

The bridegroom's mother and Mr. and Mrs. John Nason, his brother and sister-in-law returned early today from Chicago.

It was while on a 48-hour leave from his Engineer Corps outfit in 1943 that Sergeant Nason met his bride. The pair met again on subsequent leaves and decided to be married. Sergeant Nason's commanding officer approved and the wedding was set for June, 1944. Then came D-Day. The sergeant went into France. Twice he was slightly wounded, but on February 7, 1945, in Luxembourg he was wounded in the back by a German machine gun and taken to a base hospital paralyzed. He spent some time in England then was brought back to this country and to the Fort Custer Annex at Battle Creek. About 10 days ago he was transferred to the Hines hospital.

George R. Nason Jr., 49, a World War II paraplegic veteran, died on the morning of July 10, 1964 in his home, after a long illness. He was a proud, lifetime member of the Veterans of Foreign Wars.

**Figure 22. Nose Art on the B-24 bomber
"Slow Motion," somewhere in the pacific.
Photo by John Huft.**

I WAS IN LOVE WHEN THE WAR STARTED

Frances Manty
Ishpeming, Michigan

I was in love when the war started. I was 21 years old.

I, Frances Cecchini, was introduced to Martin Manty in Ishpeming, Michigan, by his cousin Bill Manty who was a friend of my best friend Rose Marra. It was easy for me to fall in love with Martin. He was easygoing, good tempered, brilliant, and a kind man. Martin was inducted into the Army and was sent to El Paso, Texas. He feared that he would be sent overseas in the war. I was left behind at home, and I worried I would never see him again. This all happened so fast.

My mother Matilda Pastori had just died at 42 years of age and I was living with my father Santé Cecchini. My father was a gardener for the Iron Ore Mines. Martin had asked me to marry him and my father told me that he thought Martin was a nice man. He gave us his support and said that I should go and marry him. Alone, I boarded a train in Ishpeming, Michigan and headed for El Paso, Texas. I was nervous and excited; nervous because I had never traveled alone anywhere and excited to go and meet with my boyfriend, the man who asked me to be his wife. The train ride took two days, and I met a very nice man, dressed in his Lieutenant's uniform, and I perceived safety in the glisten of his medals. He noticed that I was alone and nervous, and he took me under his wing and made sure I was ok; he was the proverbial officer and a gentleman. The train pulled in to the southern town of El Paso, Texas while Martin was on duty at the Army Base. The traveling Lieutenant saw to it that I found my way to the hotel where Martin had arranged for my accommodations. I was shown my room and to my dismay, when I pulled the blankets back, I found there were bugs in the bed. I clearly couldn't stay there and Martin came to my rescue, finding another place for me to stay. This Catholic girl found herself living in a home with a Methodist couple which turned out to be a very good living situation.

Martin and I were anxious to make plans to be married. We had to get approval from Martin's military command in order to get married and that was accomplished. I was Catholic and had neglected to get permission from my parish priest to get married and therefore could not be married in the Catholic Church. Martin was a Lutheran and he made arrangements for the wedding ceremony. I agreed to become a Lutheran after we were married. Under these circumstances I assumed we were being married by a Lutheran minister but it turned out we were married by a Methodist minister in the minister's home. The minister and his wife were incredibly kind to us and they hosted a reception in our honor at their home, complete with a generous supply of champagne. Drinking champagne was new to this young bride and I report that I don't remember the details of where we spent our wedding night; but, by that time my reputation remained intact and I was safe in the arms of my husband, the man I loved, and the details of where we stayed did not matter on that "memorable" evening.

Our honeymoon lasted for about one week. Then, Martin had to return to the base and I boarded a train and go back home, as there were no accommodations for military wives in El Paso. When I returned home to Ishpeming, Michigan, I lived with my father. I got a job at a garment factory making bras. I was paid piece work, but since I was a good seamstress and could work fast, I made pretty good money. I was pleased to find out that I was expecting our first child. Michael Martin Manty was born March 30, 1942. Martin was not able to come home when Michael was born, one of the sacrifices that our men in uniform experienced during the war years. He was able to come home for a few days when or son Michael was six months old. He did not see his son again until the war was over and he came home for good. Michael was almost three years of age when Martin returned home.

I worried that Martin would be going overseas. He had told me he was prepared to be shipped out at anytime; however the war came to an end and he never had to go overseas. When he came home from the war Martin went to school on the GI Bill and I continued to work in the garment industry while he went to school. He went to Northern

Michigan College in Marquette, Michigan. After he graduated from that school we moved and he went to Michigan State University where he received his Masters Degree in Vocational Rehabilitation.

We returned to Marquette, Michigan where Martin worked in his field of Vocational Rehabilitation. When our son Michael was six years old, we welcomed our second child; a daughter, Jacqueline Frances Manty born Aug 30, 1948. When Jacqueline was two years old, we moved to Battle Creek, Michigan for Martin's career. In 1968, Martin was offered a position for the State of Michigan in Traverse City, Michigan. He secured that position, we moved and he remained in that position until he retired in 1979.

Martin died in 1998. While returning home from Michigan's Upper Peninsula he had a heart attack while he was driving us across the Mackinaw Bridge. He lost control of our car as we approached the southern end of the bridge's span, no longer over the waters of the Straits of Mackinac we ended up in a field on the Lower Michigan side of the bridge. There was a group of young girls playing softball in that field and they helped me get help. Martin was transported to a hospital in Petoskey, Michigan and his unfortunate passing was confirmed to me by the doctors there. I remained in that hospital for about one week due injuries sustained to my leg.

Martin and I had a good life together. Even though distance separated us during the war years, Martin's orders as an Army Sergeant kept him stateside and he was never sent overseas. Many of Martin's friends and co-comrades were deployed overseas and we observed that things could have been very different for us if Martin if his service had included the warfront. I feel we were very fortunate.

Martin Manty was born April 28, 1919, one of seven siblings; two brothers, Walter, and Albert and four sisters, Ruth, Mildred, Alice-Jean, and Ina. I, Frances Cecchini Manty was born May 25th 1921, one of three siblings; two sisters Anna and Eleanor. I currently reside in the beautiful resort town of Traverse City, Michigan.

Figure 24. Gloria Mitchell and four other US Army WACs visit with Marlene Dietrich while Gloria is stationed with the 12th Army Group in France. Gloria is standing, second from right. Official US Army Photo provided by Mrs. Mitchell.

Figure 23. Gloria Mitchell sitting with her father examining war trophies from their respective wars. Photo from Gloria Mitchell.

Friendship Crosses Over Many Barriers

Gloria Mitchell
US Army, WAC

Since my service in World War II, I have been asked to tell my stories in various venues. I repeat a couple of these stories at this time to help recall my experiences during those years.

The first submission was to: Chicken Soup for the Veteran's Soul

Dear Sirs:

I am honored to submit my short story. It's the first story I have ever submitted to a book publisher. My children and grandchildren have been after me to write down some of my stories, so this is the first one, even if it doesn't get published.

Thanking you in advance for your consideration, I remain,

Gloria I Mitchell

Friendship Crosses Over Many Barriers

Meeting Frieda was a changing point in my life. It was shortly before the ending of WWII, in early May of 1945 that we met. Frieda was a young German girl and she had a sister Anna. They were hired by the US Army as hotel maids to serve all 88 of us WAC's that were attached to General Omar Bradley's 12th Army Group. Having a maid after living in combat conditions for 11 months, moving with the Armies, this was pure luxury.

Frieda and Anna were very sweet young ladies, always smiling and they couldn't do enough for us girls.

I often worked nights so at times I was the only one in our room when Frieda was there cleaning during the day. We didn't speak each other's language, but we could make each other understand. I looked forward to our times together. She even invited me to where she and Anna lived which was the basement of a ruined house. I explained to her that even though the war was now ended – we still couldn't fraternize with the German people and she understood.

Our friendship continued until I received my orders that I was being transferred to Frankfurt am Main, Germany.

I remember so vividly the day we left Wiesbaden. All the hotel staff was standing on the curb waving us goodbye. Just before our truck pulled away – all of a sudden there was Frieda running to our truck. She spotted me and pressed a small package into my hand. I thanked her, but couldn't imagine what it could be – maybe something to eat from the kitchen. Later when I opened it up there was this darling little black doll with its curly hair and beads around its neck. There was also a short note, which I later had translated which said, "after this is all over, could we become friends." She signed her full name and another address which was in a different part of Germany.

After I discharged and living back home again with my family, I started writing to Frieda and she wrote back. I was married 8 months later and when I returned from my honeymoon there was a letter from Frieda. Enclosed was her wedding picture. She and I were married about the same time.

My husband and I were aware of all the shortages that German people needed, so we began sending Frieda and Willie packages about once a month. When Frieda had her little girl about a year later, she wrote that the coffee we sent her helped her recover so much sooner.

As the economy improved in Germany, Frieda started sending us little thank you packages. I especially appreciated the Christmas ornaments – they were so different from ours and I still have them.

The years passed. I had two daughters and a son. Frieda had only one daughter named Ingeline.

When my oldest daughter was 16 in 1966, she and I went on a tour to Europe to visit seven countries. I wrote Frieda saying we would be in Frankfurt, Germany, on one of our stops and staying at this certain hotel and would love to see her again. I didn't receive a reply from her so I thought that it wouldn't work out for her, but what a wonderful surprise we had when we stepped off the bus – there stood Frieda and her daughter Ingeline to greet us. They looked so lovely. We hugged, kissed and cried with joy. I had to explain to everyone on our tour how Frieda and I met.

That evening at dinner our tour guide ate with us and translated for us. Suzy and Ingeline had fun singing the "Beatles" songs that were playing on the juke box. Ingeline knew all the English words.

After dinner we exchanged gifts in Frieda's room. She even had gifts for my other daughter Connie, my son Jim and my husband. Willie had a Mercedes Benz Agency and couldn't leave his business to make the long overnight train trip to meet us.

The next morning we all had breakfast together. I tried very hard to persuade Frieda and her family to come to the US to visit us. Her father-in-law lived with them and he was getting old and they couldn't leave him, so they never came.

We continued sending letters and pictures over the years. Ingeline's wedding pictures and later on pictures of her little children.

In 1975, I received in the mail a death notice from Ingeline stating that her mother had died suddenly. She was only in her early fifties.

I still have that little doll she gave me. The sawdust is slowly leaking out. Friendship crosses over many barriers. Frieda's friendship helped to soften my memories of all the terrible destruction and lives lost in this very important event that changed the course of history.

My next submission was to the *Michigan History Magazine*:

Gloria recalls Omaha Beach

An issue of "Michigan History Magazine: features the June 1944 D-Day recollections of numerous GIs including Plainwell's Gloria Mitchell shown in her WWII uniform and now with her granddaughter. In the article, Gloria states, "On June 6, 1944 I was disembarking from the *Queen Elizabeth* in Scotland along with my company of 88 WACs and hundreds of GIs not knowing that just a few weeks later our company would also land on Omaha Beach. We were known as mobile WACs and moved every few days or weeks as the invasion progressed into France and Germany. Our unit received the Normandy invasion ribbon, plus battle star."

"This June I will return to England and France to celebrate the 50th anniversary of the Normandy invasion. I want to stand on Omaha Beach again, 50 years later, and think of the 22 year old girl and all of my comrades who took part in the invasion that changed the course of world history."

**Figure 25. President Roosevelt delivering the "Day of Infamy" speech following the attack
on the naval base at Pearl Harbor and other bases on Oahu, Hawaii.
This image is a US Government photo in the public domain.**

FIVE STARS IN OUR WINDOW
Patricia Nelson
West Branch, Michigan

A day that will live in infamy! Those were the words that were spoken by President Roosevelt the day following that fateful day of December 7, 1941. It probably seemed like any other Sunday afternoon to most thirteen-year olds, but to me, it was a day of terror.

I was eighth in a family of nine. I had five older brothers, and three sisters. By age, they were Vivian, Douglas, Owen, John, Doris, Bill, Bob, Pat (myself), Roxy, and last but not least was our black Cocker Spaniel, "Corky"

My two oldest brothers were both already in the service. Douglas, the oldest, was in the Navy and Owen, the second, was in the Army. They were both stationed in California and all the newsmen were quick to announce that it was speculated that the next attack by the Japanese would be in California.

Figure 26, Patricia Nelson's five brothers. From the left: John, Owen, Bob, Doug, and Bill. Photo from Patricia Nelson.

The next few weeks, the news was hard to listen to. Then my third brother, John, enlisted in the Navy. We seldom missed a news broadcast, and every evening, my father would sit by the kitchen table and write a few lines to each of his three sons to tell them everything that was happening in our little town of West Branch. He would only mail about three letters to each one every week, but he wrote to each of them every day.

The *Bay City Times* was our main source of information. At least every week casualties were announced in the paper alphabetically. Our neighbor was one of the first casualties.

We thought we were helping the war effort with our small school's attempt at collecting papers and metal.

It was a big deal to take a quarter to school on Friday and buy a United States savings stamp. If you could squeeze out an extra quarter from time to time, things would really look up. Otherwise, it would take 75 weeks to buy a war bond for $18.75 that would be worth $25.00 in ten years. We were told that this money helped to finance the war, so we thought we were helping the war effort. We were even given a small pin to wear that said "War Gallant" How proud we were!

I earned a dollar a week counting ration stamps for the local grocery store. We separated the stamps according to meat, butter, sugar, canned foods, etc. and put each group in an envelope. Wow! I felt important! Like I was helping win the war!

On March 28, 1943, our beloved father died very suddenly and turned our lives upside down. Since we lived in the small town of West Branch, Michigan, there were not many opportunities for my mother who was suddenly the breadwinner for the family, by then twins, Bob and Bill, sixteen-years old, myself who was fifteen-years old, my sister Roxy, who was ten-years old, and of course, Corky, the dog.

My sister Vivian was the oldest of the nine of us. She had, several years before, moved to Ypsilanti, Michigan where she was able to work in a defense plant at Willow Run where they made the B-24 bomber planes. Mom went to Ypsilanti also and went to work in the same war plant. Bill, Bob and I stayed in our home and finished the school year. Roxy and Corky went to stay with an Aunt.

Ypsilanti was bulging from the influx of wartime factory workers, so all Mom could find to rent were sleeping rooms. Bob and Bill had turned seventeen so they both enlisted in the Navy. Roxy and Corky went back to live with Aunt Ellen and I went back to West Branch to work for my room and board and do my junior year of High School. Doris, my third sister, had moved to Massachusetts to marry her Navy sweetheart. There were no two members of our family in the same town except Mom and Vivian.

That year, I met a handsome soldier who was home on leave from the Army. Most of my friends had a boyfriend in service. I didn't want to be outdone, so I spent the next three years writing to him as he traveled all over Europe. On D-Day, I knew he was stationed in Africa, but I didn't know if he had been sent to France or not. I found out later that he hadn't gone to France until sometime after that.

I was going to Ypsilanti, Michigan to spend Christmas with my mother. The day before I was to leave, our family friend, Mrs. Atkins, called to tell me she had something she wanted to send to my mother. When I got to her house, she proudly announced to me that she had found a Five-star flag. It was the custom then to hang a small flag in your window with a blue star to symbolize each son that was in the service. Mrs. Atkins had two blue stars on her flag. She knew that very few families had five servicemen so five-star flags were hard to find. She also asked me to tell my mother that she had just heard from the Red Cross that her son George was alive and well as of the middle of November. She hadn't heard from him for a long time, so she contacted the Red Cross to see if they could trace to find out how he was. She happily said that now they could have a happy Christmas. On Christmas Eve 1943 they received a telegram from the war department that George had been killed in action on the island of Tarawa. It was a bad Christmas for all of us. George's blue star would then be replaced with a gold star to show that he had paid the ultimate sacrifice. Thank God, when the war ended, all the stars in our window were blue.

The following year, Mom was able to buy a small house so Roxy, Mom, I, and of course Corky were finally together again. By this time, we were able to hang our Five-Star Flag in our front window to proudly announce to the world that we had five service men in our family. Corky, of course, missed his family terribly. He would always recognize a Navy uniform and run up to greet any sailor he saw. Most of the sailors would be kind to him and pet him, but he was always disappointed that they were not his kids.

It was a difficult year for me because I had always gone to a small Catholic School with 12 members in a class, and now I was in a public school with over 100 class members. Once I was able to make friends, it was a very good school. We had lots of chances to work on different projects that we thought were helping the war effort.

The most difficult thing in our lives at that time was our constant worry about our brothers. John was serving on the USAT *George Washington*, an Army troop ship, and he crossed the Atlantic 30 times. He was a signalman first class. Douglas was a Chief Pharmacist's Mate. He spent several years in Alaska and the rest of the war on the Pacific Ocean. Bob and Bill were at sea on the Pacific, on tank landing ships (LSTs). Owen was sent to officer candidate school and got a commission. He was in the same class as Clark Gable in Miami and got to know him real well. He said Clark Gable was a very ordinary man who expected no special treatment and was liked by everyone. Owen spent the rest of the war stationed in San Antonio, Texas, where he taught new cadets their basic training before they went into preflight. He ended up making a career of the Army and retired after 30 years.

I worried about my brothers, like most sisters did, but it wasn't until I was older, and had been a wife and a mother, that I realized what it must have been like. I really feel that the unsung heroes of any war have got to be the wives and mothers of the servicemen who served overseas. We didn't have a telephone at that time, so if anybody got a leave or any other big news, they sent a telegram to Roxy, our little sister, so that when they came to announce a telegram we knew that it was not from the War Department.

My mother worked very steadily in the "Bomber Plant'". I don't remember ever hearing her complain but by the time she was 50 years old, she had snow white hair. There were quite a few boys we knew that were killed or missing in action and I think she cried for every one of them. We had several cousins who were injured and one who taken prisoner by the Germans and this was hard on her too.

On May 8, 1945, we celebrated V-E Day. This was a big day because we thought we could finally see peace in the world. The war in Japan was still pretty fierce so we still worried a lot. When we heard about the atom bomb being dropped, we were very hopeful.

On June 15, 1945, I graduated from Ypsilanti Central High School. There was not the usual celebration in our family, because we were so scattered, but Aunt Doris did come from Saginaw, so we had a special time for celebration.

In August, when the Japanese surrendered, we were so thankful! It was quite a day. It just happened that we were taking the bus to West Branch that day. It was a joyous trip. Every town that we went through was celebrating. The streets were full of people laughing and dancing. It was a day I will never forget.

It took a while for my brothers to all get home, but they were all alive and well and we knew we had been very blessed as a family. Even Corky knew he could sleep with both eyes closed now that he wasn't responsible for the safety of the whole family.

We had a joyous reunion when each of the brothers came home. Nels Nelson, my "handsome soldier" whom I had written to for three years, came home to West Branch, but of course I was then living in Ypsilanti. We really had very little in common, so the big romance ended. A few years later, we met again and dated for six months and then got married. We bought a farm and raised three fabulous children. He died suddenly of a heart attack in 1985.

Our lives had all been changed by that dreadful war. For the most part, a lot of that was good, but we were never again all together as a family. Douglas married a girl from Spokane, Washington. Owen married a girl from Minnesota. John married a girl from Chicago, Illinois. Bob married a girl from Italy and Bill married a girl from

Ypsilanti, Michigan. Vivian married a man whose family came from Italy. Doris married a man whose family came from Russia. Roxy married a man from Northern Michigan and I married a man whose family came from Sweden. We were like a small United Nations.

As a kid, I just took all the changes in our family for granted and I didn't know anything else, but now that I am older and think back, it makes me rather angry. My childhood was ripped away from me at the ripe old age of thirteen because of a world-wide war and leaving me very anti-war. I don't know that much has been accomplished by many of the wars we have seen and I think that people of the world could, and hopefully will, find a better ways to settle their differences.

Figure 27. Peter Novak's WWII medals and devices. Display provided by Peter Novak.

A PROUD US ARMY INFANTRY MAN

Peter Novak
US Army, Maple City, Michigan

I was born on July 11, 1918 on a farm in Maple City, Michigan, the son of Peter and Eva Novak and brother to Dormand, Clarence, Orpha and Betty. As a young man I worked with my family on the farm. I graduated from Maple City High School. I was drafted into the Army and left Traverse City on July 10, 1942 on a train headed towards my induction at Fort Custer, Michigan. At my physical examination, a man next to me said he could not hear. The officer dropped a coin and the man turned around to pick it up and the officer said, "You can hear." I was next and the officer said I was a perfect infantry man. I took my training at Camp Roberts, California. This training was rigorous and included daily exercise, marches, and weapons drills.

We departed the United States by boat from San Francisco on January 23, 1943. The conditions on that old Dutch boat were at some times intolerable. The latrines were unkempt. Meals were provided only twice a day. I got hungry. It was dangerous in the crow's nest; you could easily fall out and you were up there looking for the enemy. All and all I fared pretty well during the journey, but some had a very difficult cruise. One time I was able to get my hands on a few potatoes and shared them, hoping to help some seasick comrades. We arrived in the Pacific Theater on February 9,

Figure 28. Corporal Peter Novak, US Army

73

1943, landing at Guadalcanal. We scaled the boat's side on a rope with our pack and rifle on our back, lowering down to a barge in the water, out about a mile from shore. On the island we set up camp, always on alert for lizards, alligators and wild pigs. I later participated in the Bougainville and the New Georgia campaigns.

As we went into battle, a fellow soldier was injured. I was selected to see that he got onto a medical Jeep and transported to the field hospital. During this attempt, we were ambushed and had to stay for the night. I took the wounded soldier to the bomb hole and prepared him for the night. I dug my foxhole before dark. The enemy located us, and the soldier in the bomb hole was killed. As for me, the enemy walked over me. I was sure he found me. I had my bayonet but no success. The enemy walked on. When the enemy left, they shelled the area and one landed close to my feet. It stunned me, and after I came to, I found three soldiers that were still able to help and we took our wounded comrades to the 147th Infantry Regiment. From Guadalcanal we went to Bougainville where the enemy troops were waiting for us. I carried a Browning Automatic Rifle, the infamous BAR, as we moved forward. The artillery shelled us. One hit about six feet behind me and it blew me up into a banana tree. My fellow soldiers knew I was in the area, so they searched and found me up in the tree. They sent me to the field hospital and there they removed all the shrapnel that they could. I went to the New Hebrides and was sent back to the States via airplane to California. Due to my injuries, I was assigned a nurse to travel with me and we were escorted by medical staff to care for me and the other wounded soldiers.

I was honorably discharged on November 9, 1944, in Indiana. I earned and received the following medals: Purple Heart, Good Conduct, WWII Victory, Asiatic-Pacific, Bronze Star, Infantry Combat, American Campaign, and Infantry Marksman. I have kept these medals and still have them in my possession today, framed and proudly displayed.

After the war, I worked at Part's Manufacturing Co. (PMC) as a tool crib operator. After PMC closed, I worked at Munson Medical Center (MMC), starting in the laundry area. I left MMC to work as a dental technician building dentures. After ten years, I rejoined the workforce at MMC, working as a boiler operator and in maintenance. I retired from Munson Medical Center in 1987.

When I returned from military service, I reunited with Mary Shetteck, the girl that waited for me while I was in the Army. We were married on September 28, 1946 at St. Rita's in Maple City, Michigan and we have been married for 63 years. Mary and I had six sons, a very nice family; Dan born in 1948, Gary born in 1952, John born in 1954, Duane born in 1957, Mark born in 1962, and Loren born in 1965. We have five grandchildren: Scott, Troy, Michael, Natalie and Nathan. We have two great-grandchildren: K.C. and Leah. Mary and I are blessed with a great family.

Figure 29. A PBD destroyed in an air attack on Henderson Field, Guadalcanal in 1942. Official U.S. Navy Photograph, now in the collections of the National Archives

Figure 30. General Dwight D. Eisenhower addresses American paratroopers the day before D-Day. These men each boarded their aircraft and they were on the ground in France before the landings on Normandy's beaches. US Army Photograph, in the public domain.

REVEILLE TO TAPS: EVERYDAY AN ADVENTURE
Chauncey (Dick) Nunnelley
US Army Air Forces, Birmingham, Michigan

Reveille - Orientation

I enlisted in Detroit, Michigan in the Army Air Forces on November 18, 1942. On the same day, we shipped out to Fort Custer for the first part of an orientation. We were outfitted with uniforms, etc. The only thing we could take with us was a small bag with personal items.

At Fort Custer we were given a "bank" of tests. This was to determine what branch of the Army Air Forces we would be assigned to. When I was called in, the officer said I rated high on mechanical ability and that I was being assigned to Keesler Air Force Base in Biloxi, Mississippi. In a couple of days others, and I, were assigned to Keesler Field and were put on a train. The next stop was on a railroad siding in Chicago. This just happened to be next to a rendering plant - a great way to start a career. We were there about a full day while they made up the rest of the train.

Upon arriving at Keesler Field, we were started on our orientation. This lasted a couple of days. It was explained what we would be doing. Namely, we would be in school every day for the next six months. Each day we would be in a different classroom, studying a B-24 bomber. At the completion of our schooling we would be classified as a crew chief maintaining B-24's. And so with that we started school. By the way, it was an excellent course of instruction and it took up the entire six months of training. At the completion, we were given corporal stripes and a certificate stating we were crew chiefs. Next was a train ride back to Romulus, Michigan to the Ford bomber plant. There we were placed on the assembly line building B-24s right along side of the workers.

A couple of weeks went by and the plane I was assigned to was nearing completion. As it approached the huge doors at the end of the line there was an officer standing there with a clipboard. (By the way, everyone has a clipboard). He asked me my name and number. I have already learned that I'm going to repeat this many times over the next three years. *"C.G. Nunnelley Corporal, 15-16-9640 SIR."* He said, "Corporal, this is your plane and you are to follow it wherever it goes." Note there were no written orders, just verbal directions, leaving plenty of questions. The plane was rolled out to the flight line with many others (there were 19,000 B-24's made in four plants).

On the flight line, the "clipboard" squad inspectors took over. Each person, with clipboard in hand, started inspecting each and every one of the several thousand parts which made up the B-24. I followed each one watching what they were doing. The second or third day we had a serious accident on the plane next to mine. It was night, dark, and raining and a lady inspector came on the plane to inspect an item. She completed her inspections, exited the plane by the bomb door, jumped off the catwalk, threw her raincoat over her head and ran forward instead of aft and ran right into the back of a revolving propeller. Needless to say, what happened was very sad.

My plane was nearing being ready for a test flight and they were assigning test pilots to each completed plane. The well known flyer, Charles Lindbergh was being assigned, and I was hoping he would get my plane, but I missed him by one plane. (It would have been nice story to tell your grandchildren).

Firearms Training

When my plane was ready, another officer got the group together and sent us all to Minnesota for firearms orientation. While we were gone for three days, my plane was sent to Big Spring, Texas. I was supposed to be on it, so I had to hitch a ride with another crew and I went to Big Spring, Texas. Remember, the only orders I had were to follow this plane wherever it goes. The only thing I could think of was what does AWOL mean? In Big Spring they said that the plane went to Liberal, Kansas. So, I got another ride. I found out that it blew a nose wheel on landing and that means it is scrapped. So, I was assigned to their headquarters group until my orders caught up with me. That meant painting rocks around sidewalks, picking up cigarette butts from airmen who didn't know how to "field strip." Oh well, time passed and my orders caught up with me and I got assigned to Group 4 as Crew Chief with seven mechanics. This did not last long as I started flying as Crew Chief/Flight Engineer. This lasted about 2 ½ years during which I flew 1,400 hours.

First Flight

My first flight caused me to wonder what was ahead. When we took off, we went a few miles from the base and dropped down to about 1,000 feet above the ground and stayed there (or lower). The pilot "buzzed" every farmer on a tractor for miles around. We were flying for about two and one half hours. At that time, no one had identification marked on their plane. The order went out and the painters went to work painting six foot numbers on every plane. "That stopped the buzzings."

Figure 31. Crew Chief Chauncey Nunnelley

Many Routine Days Flying

The job of the Crew Chief/Flight Engineer was to maintain the B-24 in flying condition. If there were problems with the plane, you needed to let the pilot know about it. For instance, I had one plane in my group that had been on observation duty in the Gulf of Mexico. They modified it by putting a big plastic bubble in place of a turret on the nose, for observers. The plane was not airworthy. A major came out with his two students and we were ready for takeoff. He leaned to one student and said, "Today, we are going to practice a three-engine take-off." Hearing that, I said to the major, "This aircraft will not take off on three engines." He looked at me as if to say "what sergeant can tell a major that he can't take off with only three engines."

In order to simulate this procedure, you pull back on an inboard engine to 850 revolutions per minute (RPMs). This is one time I strapped in, because I knew I was in for a "good ride." We got to the last intersection and did not have enough air speed to lift the plane off of the runway. With that, he put the engine up to get airworthy then made a mistake. He pulled it back again and we hit the ground. He had made another mistake but got lucky because he had not raised the landing gear. At this point he put power on with all four engines, we lifted off again, he turned and looked at me and I gave him a sick smile. It is the flight engineer's duty to keep the pilot aware of problems on the plane. I never flew with him again and the radioman who was on board when we landed said he wanted to get out. We let him.

Trip to Rest Camp

There was a Civilian Conservation Corps (CCC) Camp in the mountains outside Laramie, Wyoming and we used it as a rest camp for personnel from Liberal Air Force Base. When you were sent there for about ten days, you were on your own. The only staff there were two cooks; they would prepare breakfast and lunch. That was all. However, the cooks would rotate duty there for about two weeks. So, they needed to be flown up there. My plane was assigned to make the trip. I was checking it out and two cooks showed up and said they were to be flown up to the camp. I asked them if they had flown before. Neither had. I told them as soon as I checked the plane out that I would be with them. I took them in and showed them where they would ride. I explained how to use the parachutes and explained how to bail out if the jump button signal went off. I then went up to the flight deck. We took off and I checked with them a few times. Later in the flight I noticed that the pilot was "playing" with the jump button. You cannot hear this on the flight deck. I ran to the back and they had opened the hatch and were kneeling down, ready to roll out. I yelled at them, "Don't jump!" They stood up and breathed a sigh of relief. With this, I went up to the pilot and explained what had happened. If he had held down on the button for a short time, we would have lost two cooks. We were directly over the Rocky Mountains. We would have never found them.

When you were at the camp, the only rule was to inform someone at the camp where you were going. Storms would come over the mountain and you would get lost quickly. The mountain directly behind the camp had an elevation of 8,000 feet.

Shifts of Flying

For the most part we were flying three shifts a day, starting with morning around 8:00 a.m. Generally, if you were scheduled to go cross-country, to any place in the United States, you flew the 8:00 a.m. shift and you could be gone for three or four days. The afternoon shift started around 1:00 p.m. What that shift called for was "shooting" landings, which were also called "touch & go" landings. It was nothing to land about 30 times in the afternoon. The pilot would fly a pattern, land, power on (without stopping). Each time he did that, the flight engineer had to go through the bomb bay, open the waist gun windows, and make sure the landing gear was down and locked, and then go back up and inform the pilot it was safe to land. Do this 30 times in an afternoon and you get a good workout. Then there was the night shift. This involved navigation and watching out for other planes. One time we were taking off on a dual runway. The pilots and the flight engineer are very familiar with all lights on the horizon, and just after takeoff I noticed a light I did not recognize. A few seconds later I put my hand on the shoulder of the student pilot, who was at the controls, and said to him, "Hard left." With that he banked the plane hard to the left. What I saw was the left elevator of another B-24 that we were overtaking. The light I saw was located just above the identification number on the tail of another slower B-24. Those numbers were on the stabilizer tail so you had to be pretty close to read it. The student pilot beside me, who was not flying the plane, said "I saw it at the same time you did and I couldn't talk." I said, "That's what we are here for." Then my guts quieted down. That was a close call.

Gas Leak

The flight engineer (especially at night) takes a full trip through the plane making sure there are no gas or fluid leaks, or any other problems. On a routine walk through, I noticed what appeared to be a gas leak. The gasoline had a dye in it that caused traces of leaks to show up. I notified the pilot and said I would keep an eye on it. The next time it looked like it was a little wetter, so I said to the pilot that I think we better take the plane in. He said, "Dear God," and they changed course and got into the landing pattern. In the meanwhile, I took up a position so I could watch the leak closely. I turned off the hydraulic pump so that it would not spark when the brakes were applied. Just as we hit the runway, the leak let go and dumped gasoline in the bomb bay. I yelled up to the pilot. I told him we had a bad leak and that when he put on the brakes to keep them on, do not pump them, and that when we stop I will put on the strap that holds the brakes on and then hit the crash bar for killing all power. I would open the bomb doors and we would exit the plane that way. Things went well and the fire crew said the next day that we lost 500 gallons of gasoline on the runway. Close call.

A Planned Cross Country

After a heavy December snow storm, there were 25 B-24s lined up to take off and do their flying out of another air base that did not have the snowfall we had. Of the 25 planes lined up, we were #3. Plane #1 crashed on 17 left taking that runway out of service. Plane #2 took off on runway 17 right. We lined up on 17 right, and in applying power, our #4 supercharger ran away and we landed hard on 17 right. We lost our #1 engine, the left nose wheel was torn off the landing gear, and the left wing was down to the ground. We opened the flight deck hatch and exited by running down the left wing to the ground. When we got down, one student pilot was not accounted for. So, I ran up the wing, looked in and he was putting on his shoes. I said, "Get the hell out of there; we've got gasoline all over the place." Well, that was all three runways closed so 22 planes turned around and went back to the ramp. That afternoon the runways were cleared up and we all took off. We spent the next five days flying out of Dallas, Texas.

Trip to Fresno, California

We were taking six pilots who had completed their training out to Fresno for an assignment. So we were flying over the Grand Canyon. The instructor turned to me and asked, "What's that building on the edge of the canyon." I said, "If my information is correct, the Santa Fe railroad built it for their employees for a retreat that they could go to at a reasonable price and so forth." He said, "I think we'd better buzz that." I didn't say anything to him, because that's his privilege, he is the Commander. We flew west a little bit and turned around and came down to a buzzing level. We got to the edge of the canyon, and he put it in the down position. We went into the canyon but when I say into the canyon we were at the ridge elevation. Then he tried to turn and the air was very soft for some reason. We turned and headed straight for the canyon wall. And, he turned to me and he said, "Chief, when I tell you, give me full flaps." Well, when the flaps come down it changes the configuration on the wind going over the wing. And so, when he said "Now," I put it in the down position and the plane changes its attitude, and the tail comes up and the nose goes down, raising the plane over the canyon wall. When this was behind us, we got out and I raised the flaps up. The only thing that was said was when he turned to me and said, "Boy, did I ever grow up today." Well, it was close to a major disaster. We had six pilots in the back and four of us in the front. So that was it. It's worth telling.

Oh, one last story, I've got plenty of them. I've got more stories than you've got time.

Cross Country Scheduled

My plane was scheduled to go on a cross-country to Louisville, Kentucky which was only 60 miles from Lexington, Kentucky, my hometown. I came out in the morning and started up the engines and got them up to heat and so forth - it isn't uncommon for the flight engineer to start the engines. I was just getting out of the pilot's seat when the pilot and two students came on. The pilot said, "Stay there, Chief." I was known as Crew Chief and Flight Engineer, so you get called anything. And, I said, "Ok." He said, "Start 'em up." I put the radioman out on the firewatch and started 'em up and I looked at the pilot again with that, "You want this pilot or your student in the seat?" He said, "No, taxi out." So I said, "Ok." So, I let the radio man get up and stand right where the turret was. We had a hatchway there. He got up and stood so he could watch the wingtips so they didn't get too close to anything. By the way, we took those turrets out on modification time and put sheet metal over that, because this was a training plane and that's a good place to introduce this. The Liberal Air Force Base's lone objective was to take students that had their wings and send them to Liberal to learn to fly B-24s so that all the time they were there they were being taught to fly B-24s. Some of them could fly and some of them had difficulty. So anyway, I taxied out to the runway and asked if he wanted me to run 'em up? He said, "Yup." You always have a checklist and you have to go through that conscientiously. You read off everything and you do that operation right there, like testing the cowling, etc. He said, "Well, let's get out on the runway." I said, "Call the tower and get permission." He said, "Ok," and he got permission to head up. We lined up on the runway, fully expecting him to call for another student. Now he says, "Take off!" I said, "Ok," so I proceeded to take off. I got up to about 110 MPH and lifted off and pulled back on the columns and we got up to about 6,000 feet. I said, "Where do you want to fly?" He said, "About 8,000 feet." So, I took it up to 8,000 feet. Then he smiled, knowing full well that I knew nothing about navigation, and said, "Take me to Louisville, Kentucky." At that point, I wasn't going to be beaten down, and I said, "Ok." I reached up and turned on the radio compass and I said, "Find the radio station for St. Louis." So he found the station and the needle came around just like that and what you do then is just follow the needle. So, I followed it to St. Louis and it all of a sudden went the other way around and I said, "Now get radio station WHAS in Louisville." To make a long story short, I flew all the way to Louisville and set down there, flew all the way back to Liberal and set down there. That was an interesting flight. That was one of the reasons that we couldn't go overseas, because we were taught to fly and we had the responsibility to fly with the students on their "solo" flights.

Cable Repair

One interesting thing happened here. I was getting ready to go home on my first furlough when I was to get married and I had redone the flight cables on the plane. Flight cables control the plane from the column back to the rudders, elevators, ailerons, etc. I had completed all of those and I called for a test pilot to come out and test it. And, they came out and we got it in the air, went through all the maneuvers and tested all the controls on it. He said, "Looks pretty good chief. Let's give it the ultimate test." So, we went up to about 8,000 feet and he pushed forward on the column and down we went. We were losing altitude at 1,500 feet a minute and doing probably close to 300 miles per hour. So anyway, he pulled back on the column and he said, "You did a good job, that's good." And I said, "Take me back up, I can't hear anything." He said, "That'll go away." I said, "I don't think so." But, I had to go along with him, you can't order him to do it… you can order him down if something is wrong but you can't order him up. So anyway, we landed; I got back and couldn't hear anything. I got on the train the next morning to come to Detroit to get married and they had the long ceremony planned where you exchange vows and all that and I said, "We can't do it, I can't hear anybody." And so, we went through the short ceremony, and when it got to the part where I was supposed to say "I do," my wife jabbed me and I said, "I do!" They swore it was all legal, but anyway I was that way during my whole furlough and my whole honeymoon trip, but when I was running to catch a train in Chicago, my hearing broke loose. Holy mackerel, I thought the world was coming to an end. And, so it was interesting.

I have been asked how the food was and did you feel stressed at all? The food was good. It kept you alive. When we were flying and we landed on some air bases, maybe it was after dark or something.

We could always go to the main lunch room or dining hall and they would fix dinner for us.

There were times when I felt pressure and stress. A lot of these flights, I'm telling you, were stressful. One that I really hated on the training, they put an imaginary wall out in the center of the runway and that's supposed to represent a wall of about 50 ft. high. With full power on, from the end of the runway, you're supposed to get the plane over that obstacle. It's one that I didn't like, because what happens is you get into that position of right over that wall and if you lose it you're done, you're gonna go down. So, you're hanging there on the props. We made it every time but some didn't. Now, at that base in that three year period, we lost 100 B-24s and 160 airmen, just in training (not all in the procedure I just mentioned).

With regard to gestures or items used for good luck; none really. I always carried a box of chocolate cookies in case I got to feeling ill, because that's how I ended up in the hospital a few times. We'd get in a really bad storm and the Crew Chief or Flight Engineer was never strapped in. He'd go up and hit the ceiling and then hit the floor. One time when we were flying over Wichita, and we had the two student pilots, the radio man and all three had their heads into the bomb bay and upchucking, they were really sick. So, I got up to the pilot and said, "We've got three pretty sick people back here." Well, the student who was flying said, "I don't feel too good either." So the pilot/commander said, "Get the hell out of the seat." One of the things you have to do in flying is if you make a mess, you clean it up. Doesn't make any difference what the rank is, it could be a general, they have to clean it up. So, I got into the seat and the instructor pilot said, "You handle the radio and I'll see if I can get this thing in." Well, we managed to land at Wichita and they had a lot of cleaning up to do. That's not one of the more pleasant stories.

Well, I got one other one. I had a pilot that every time he came out he had to answer nature's call. I was flying somebody else's plane. Now on my plane I had put in a latrine, so they knew it. So, when this pilot got on, we'd be airborne and he said, "I'm going back to the back." I said, "Ok." So this one time pretty soon he came back up and said, "This isn't your plane." I said, "No," we had to fly another plane. Well, he said, "What am I gonna do?" I said, well there's an old map case back there, you can open that up and crap in that. And, once you get through, (we were over farms) just raise the hatch and throw it out. Next thing I know, he came up and said, "You got any rags?" What had happened was that he had raised the hatch up but he didn't open the wind deflector. So when he threw that map case out, it came back in, so he had to clean that up. If you've ever seen the interior of one of these planes, they're just ribs, ribs of steel. When we got down, he had to get out there and clean all that out. Well, so much for my stories.

Off Duty Entertainment

I'll give you a little secret. Before I enlisted, I was studying vocal music with the Detroit Conservancy, and I picked up a professor for private lessons. I was studying with him. I was doing wakes and weddings, etc. When I got into the service that career was out. But, Liberal was a base big enough to have a marching band. Well, out of that marching band they had at least 8 to 14 musicians that had been members of the big bands. I happened to hear them one day and they were fantastic. So, I went up to the leader and I said, "How about auditioning for a male singer for your dance band?" He said, "Ok." I said, "I haven't got any music with me." He said, "Don't worry, what do you want to sing?" I said, "Well, 'Laura' or 'White Cliffs of Dover,' they're all being done right now." So, they picked out "Laura" and they just right away played it. I auditioned there and then and they hired me that night. So, I sang when I wasn't flying. And there were other people in the band that had other duties. Nearly every night, you had between eight and fourteen members in the dance band. We did gigs all over the place. The newspapers caught the story and I got to be known as the "Swoon Crooner." Of course, that was the time of Crosby, Sinatra and Dick Ames. So, I picked up a little change and sang with the band for about two years. When Bob Hope and Les Brown and His Band of Renown came to the base, we played the warm-up set for them.

Did I pull any pranks? I'm sure I did. I was known as a prankster. I can think of a couple that I still won't tell you!

I've flown into almost every major airport in the United States. There was one airport that I didn't care to go into; that was Salt Lake City. Because, in Salt Lake City you came over the Rockies and you did a dive because roughly the airport was right there. Flying in there always made for a most memorable flight.

Engine Fire

We were on a cross country flight to Detroit and an inboard engine caught fire over Kansas City, Missouri. The extinguisher in the engine put the fire out, but we sat down in Kansas City to check it out. A fire like that calls for an engine change. We were told to stay in Kansas City. The pilots called for a plane to pick up everyone except the crew chief. So, I called Oklahoma and had them send an engine and crew to assist in the engine change. That change took 15 days. At completion, I called for pilots and when they landed they had broken a fuel pump shaft. (That's an engine change.) The crew chief on that plane could not stay, so guess who was spending another 15 days? When you are away from your base, the Red Cross allowed you to borrow $5.00 a day. So, each day we had to go to them for something to eat.

Miscellaneous

The officers and fellow crew members were all good, pretty much so. They taught you to fly, the instructors I mean. I had one officer who was a flight engineering officer that was kind of the head muckety-muck for our group. He put out a memo one day. That memo said that flight engineers will be sure that their Auxiliary Power Unit (APU) container of gasoline will be stowed and strapped in. Well, our group always put it under the waist gun floor. You could take that can, put it in there and push it down underneath that floor and it didn't go anyplace. He happened to come for a flight on my plane, I had not done that. So, I got on that plane and I was a sergeant, and when I got off, I was a private.

My flight book was a sort of personal diary. All of the things I've been talking about were highlighted in that log. But, it wasn't a diary. It was a flight log; the number of the plane, who the pilot was, etc.

Recalling the Day Service Ended

Not that it was memorable. We had been moved around a number of times. Actually, when I left Liberal Air Force Base, I was then assigned to the Third Ferrying Group. The Third Ferrying Group would pick us up in a C-47 and fly us to Oregon. Each crew was three people; the Pilot, Co-pilot and the Flight Engineer. When you got there you were to fly one of the planes that had been flown overseas; and they truly were wrecks. I mean, they left a lot to the imagination because the three of you had to take that plane and fly it to Arizona to a salvage yard. When we checked things out, it was not uncommon for us to fly a plane all the way down there with the only instruments they had were a needle ball and air speed and that's really going back to the basics of flying. They would pick us up, take us up again to Oregon and come back for more. I don't know how many flights we made. I was concerned about flying these planes, I was concerned all the time because they were just un-airworthy and we shouldn't have been flying them. But, one kind of humorous thing happened on the C-47. In the plane, we were all four engine crews, and of course the C-47 is a two engine plane. When we would get on, we would put our chutes in the aisle-way and then sit down on the bench seat. If the pilot had to feather one of the props, which means that when you feather a prop, you turn it so the wind is going right by the prop and that way if the engine has gone bad, you can still land. And so, when somebody said they lost half their engines, we all said ya that's true and would reach down and get their chute out and put it on.

I left the service and went back to Birmingham, Michigan. I then got jobs at a number of factories and machine shops. Finally, an opening happened in the fire service in Birmingham and so I put my application in and started my career in the fire service. I worked as Lieutenant, Captain and after sixteen years I was made Chief and was

Chief for 16 years. (But that's a whole new story.) I retired from that in 1979.

Post War

I remember that when my wife came to visit we had to get a room in town at a hotel or maybe an apartment house that was renting out a room or something.

I didn't take advantage of school benefits. Not that I stopped learning, I just didn't take advantage of the formal training.

I did have close friends in the service; there were three of us. There was a fellow from Cleveland, Ohio there was one from Brooklyn, New York and there was me from Birmingham, Michigan. There were three of us that were together most of the time; except on the weekends. The fellow from Brooklyn was Jewish, I was Christian, and the other one was Catholic. Since the service I have lost track of these relationships.

I have not joined any veteran's organizations. I did stay in the fire department after the war for the duration of my 32 years in the fire services. After that, I served eight years as executive director of the Home Builders Association in Traverse City, Michigan; one year as director of the Off Shore Race; and the Blue Angels.

I don't believe my military service influenced my thinking about war or the military in general. I'm broad minded. Sure it affected my life. I learned a lot when I went through that school, which was an excellent school for six months. I went to school for six months to learn hydraulics and all those things. And, they were all things that I could use outside. I have no thoughts/comments on the wars since WWII and the current war in Iraq or Afghanistan.

I've told these stories so often over the years that they just roll off. I tell ya, I feel that I was in the lost squadron. Because, I'd get together with some veteran's, veteran air people, and they would come back after being on 50 missions, etc., and we'd get together and I'd ask how may hours they put in and they wouldn't know. I've flown 1400 hours in the B-24 and I didn't get any missions. I was all over the United States.

TAPS - In Closing

My whole tour of duty was spent in the United States. There was enough "action" and challenge to what we were assigned to do.

I want to give a word of appreciation to John Kelly and his daughters for the idea of putting these experiences on paper. So, thank you very much. Hope you enjoy!

Figure 32. U.S. Army Air Forces Consolidated B-24D Liberator. U.S. Air Force photo.

Figure 33. Seabees lay pierced plank under flood lights to build an airfield on Adak in the Aleutians, Alaska. US Navy photograph.

MY STORY: A NURSING CAREER
Barbara Osborne
Houston, Texas

I am a seventy one year old, Registered Nurse currently working summers at Interlochen Arts Camp in their "Boy's Infirmary." I have also been a resident at the Village at Bay Ridge for the past three years, and that is how I have gotten involved in "my story."

I was born in 1938 in Houston, TX and lived there until I was 37 years old. The only connection I have with WWII is a few memories that have stayed with me throughout the years. My step-father, Aubry B. Fisk, was in the Navy Seabees as an electrician and his rank is unknown. He, his three brothers and his father were co-owners of the Fisk Electric Company in Houston, Texas. He married my mother in 1941 and in 1942 he enlisted in the Seabees and was part of the 12th Naval Construction Battalion. He often mentioned Kodiak, Alaska but I have no knowledge of other stations of duty. Some recent research indicates that he was later also attached to the Third Marine Raiders elsewhere in the Pacific Theater.

One memory of the war I have was when I was about four or five years old. In Houston we had frequent "air raid drills." During each drill, my mother would run out of the house at night with a blanket to cover the cement bench in the back yard, thinking that the reflections from the moonlight would be a problem. The other memory I have is about my grandmother, Ruth. She had been "seeing" a man that owned and ran a meat market. I knew that meat was rationed and that stamps were needed to purchase the meat. My family had been getting the meat from my grandmother, who had been getting it from this man she was seeing. My grandmother married another man and my mother said I was standing at the front door of my home crying as the couple drove away for their honeymoon and I was saying, "Where are we going to get meat now?"… I was five years old at the time.

While I was in High School I did volunteer work at Texas Children's Hospital, thus my interest in becoming a nurse. I entered The Methodist Hospital School of Nursing in 1956, right out of high school and graduated in 1959 with a diploma in nursing. My first job as a Registered Nurse (RN) was in Dr. Michael DeBakey's first Cardiovascular Intensive Care Unit. Dr. DeBakey and Dr. Denton Cooley had had a "falling out" at that time. Dr. Cooley, a very kind man, left Methodist Hospital and went next door to the Texas Children's Hospital and operated on babies with hearts as small as a walnut. I worked with patients that had many different surgeries: aortic aneurysms, carotid artery blockage, heart valve malfunctions, and other serious vascular problems. This was prior to the invention of the mechanical heart and heart transplants. Dr. DeBakey was much revered, not only for his skill as a cardiac surgeon, but in his final years as Chancellor of Baylor College of Medicine.

I've had many interesting experiences as an RN, but my first one in the ICU was probably the most memorable. I have worked two years as an office nurse for an OB-GYN physician while my husband, Lee Bolin, finished his last two years at Texas A & M Agriculture and Mechanical College; two years in Sacramento, California while my husband was seeking his fortune; three years in Labor and Delivery and one year as an OB supervisor. I then spent six months going through a very difficult Cardiovascular Nurse Specialist class that included on-the-job training plus class work. Following that, I worked in Intensive Care for two years. I divorced Lee at that time after fourteen years and two daughters later.

My first daughter had been born in 1963. Lynn Bolin is married and currently living in Cape Town, South Africa. She is head of marketing and media for Old Mutual, an insurance and financial company. She was Valedictorian at Port Huron Northern High School, attended Kalamazoo College and was given a full scholarship for two years at Princeton University for her Masters Degree. Princeton then gave her an all expense paid year to study in Paris, France at a government school. She has traveled around the world with her husband, David Norris who is a commercial real estate property buyer and salesman in Cape Town.

My second daughter, born in 1967, Dana Goodwin, has two boys, 11 year old Kevin and 9 year old Carson. She attended Michigan State University for her undergraduate degree and Eastern Michigan University working on her Master's degree. She is currently teaching art in the Montessori program at Glen Loomis Elementary School. She is also a professional photographer, living here in Traverse City.

I left Methodist Hospital in 1970 and went to work at the Memorial Hospital in the Coronary Care Unit in Downtown Houston, Texas. There I met the love of my life…a patient. Bob had flown down to Houston from Detroit for an Automotive Engineer's meeting and was staying at the hotel across the street from the hospital. He worked as a research chemist at the Tech Center in Warren, Michigan. He had a heart attack and ended up in my Coronary Care Unit. After five years, many visits and many phone calls later, Bob flew down to Houston from Detroit and drove me and my two young daughters back to Michigan. We were married in November 1975 and lived in Port Huron right on the lake, just north of the Blue Water Bridge for 10 years until Bob retired. By that time, my older daughter had graduated from Kalamazoo College and my younger one from high school. All during those ten years, I worked in the Coronary Care Unit at the hospital in Mt. Clemens, Michigan. I also took the time to get my bachelor's degree in nursing at the University of Detroit, graduating *Summa Cum Laude*.

Bob decided to retire after 29 years at General Motors and in 1976 we moved to Corpus Christi, Texas. There I found my favorite job, working in a Cardiac Rehab Center where I spent an additional 20 years. I met many wonderful friends, both patients and nurses, whom I continue to visit every spring since moving back to Michigan. In 1989 I saw an advertisement in a nursing journal for a nurse to work at Interlochen Arts Camp for the summer. I applied over the phone and the supervisor hired me. Bob and I drove up every summer for 17 years for me to work as a nurse in the infirmary and for him to do volunteer work at the camp; another wonderful job that I continue to do even though my love is no longer with me. Yes, here I am in Traverse City. Bob grew ill in 1996, and I wanted to be close to family. My daughter Dana, after graduating from Michigan State, moved to Traverse City. So, here I am. Bob died in March, 2007, just 10 months after moving to Traverse City. I love where I am living. I love the new friends I have made and will continue to make. I have had a wonderful life and career.

Figure 34. US troops in the harsh winter of Bastogne, Belgium, December 1944.
Photo from the US Army Signal Corps Collection, USAMHI.

WORLD WAR II MEMOIR – WRITTEN IN JULY 2009

James Preuett
US Navy, Traverse City, Michigan

My Naval travels with the USS *Catoctin* (AGC-5) – A communications ship and the flagship of Vice Admiral H.K. Hewitt for the Atlantic and Mediterranean fleets in 1944 during World War II. This memoir reflects upon portions of service time James E. Preuett spent with the U. S. Navy during World War II. My assignment was in the radar and the printing field, where many maps and specialized information were needed. Our big military assignment was to the Soviet Union for the Yalta Conference in 1945.

Following military training, I was assigned to an operations and communication headquarter ship, the USS *Catoctin*. These specialized ships – only 14 in the Navy were named after mountains – The *Catoctin* was named after the mountain range in Maryland where Camp David is located.

I received my basic training in Great Lakes, Illinois. After this training period, six other new sailors and I were sent to Norfolk, Virginia for training in the Amphibious Section. After six weeks of this training, our next stop was to Boston, Massachusetts where we received additional training in our future field of printing and photography. From Boston, we went to another school in Atlantic City, NJ, to receive more specialized training in our field of radar. Then, we traveled to Philadelphia, Pennsylvania for

Figure 35. EM3 James Preuett, US Navy.

more training and to wait for our next assignment.

We soon learned we would be assigned to the USS *Catoctin*, which was then located in Naples, Italy, serving as flagship for Commander, 8th Fleet. Naples was where the ship was based. To get to Naples, we were assigned to a seaplane tender, the USS *Humbolt (AVP-21)*, which carried us on a portion of our trip to the USS *Catoctin*.

On the seaplane tender, we were assigned work areas to help us on our trip. I was placed on the ship's lookout…scanning the area ahead for any other ships or submarines that had surfaced.

Early one morning, I was in the head getting ready for my daily watch duty when the ship had a loud bang and it felt like it lifted the ship two to three feet above the water. I grabbed my life jacket and started out to the deck. I thought the ship had been hit by a torpedo, but later learned the ship had sounding sonar and a depth charge had been dropped because of sonar soundings and readings. I hung onto my dog tags, but everything turned out well.

After crossing the Atlantic Ocean, we stopped in the Fayaz Islands in the Azores for the fuel and supplies we needed. After leaving this area, we headed to England – going up the Bristol River to the city of Bristol. This river could only be traveled while the tide was in. It was a beautiful trip up the river with high banks on each side. We spent three days there, so we could have liberty at Bristol and nearby Bath.

The next segment of our trip was to North Africa, docking at the city of Casablanca, Morocco. At this point, we departed from the seaplane tender and put ashore at a Navy camp at this North African port. After several days, we were put on a relic train car for our next assignment, which was in the city of Oran, Algeria. The camp at Oran was mostly tents, and when it rained it was a big mess. While on the train to Oran we had to post guards at our entrances to prevent the natives from grabbing our luggage and quickly leaving with our personal belongings. The train moved slowly and stopped often along the way.

The next portion of our trip was by landing craft to Sicily, Italy and then on to Naples where we joined our ship. While being assigned to a bunk on the *Catoctin*, I was told I would have to sleep in the brig, as no other bunks were available. I said, "Ok" but made sure the door was open and not locked. A few days later, we were called and advised we were getting an R&R trip to Rome, Italy for three days. This incredible trip allowed us to see and witness the areas and take in the places we learned about in school. I was able to visit Vatican City and had a visit with the Pope.

I had purchased several items, which the Pope blessed for me. I also visited the Coliseum and the ruins of Pompeii. After returning to the ship, we had several small trips to the surrounding areas including the Isle of Capri. We greatly enjoyed the beautiful Mediterranean areas we visited.

Later we learned we were going to Sicily and would go into dry dock to scrape and paint the ship. This was done in the rain, which created a big mess and lasted for three days. Also at this time, a new gangplank was installed with 3" runners on both outer edges. This caused us to wonder why the runners were needed on both sides, but we soon learned it was to push a prominent visitor, President Franklin Delano Roosevelt, aboard in a wheelchair.

After completing this work, we returned to our home base in Naples, Italy for a couple of weeks. It was there that we learned of our next assignment. We were going to Istanbul, Turkey to pick up some visitors. After another short wait, we were advised we were headed to the Soviet Union for the Yalta Conference at the Crimea vacation area.

While in Istanbul, we picked up President Franklin Delano Roosevelt and his daughter; Winston Churchill and his daughter; and Averill Harriman and his daughter, all of whom were to be transported to the Yalta Conference.

We crossed the Black Sea with five minesweepers clearing the path before us. After crossing the Black Sea, we docked at Sevastopol. The Yalta Conference was held at the Russian Summer Palace located in the Crimea vacation area some 30 miles from our base at

Sevastopol. The Crimea was a beautiful area located on the Black Sea. Each day, a motorcade made a trip through the winding road up the mountains to the Yalta Conference area at the Crimea Summer Palace. This compound was composed of several buildings with a large Summer Palace building with beautiful landscaping and a wonderful view of the mountains and the Black Sea. The Summer Palace was a very solid, large and beautiful two-story building.

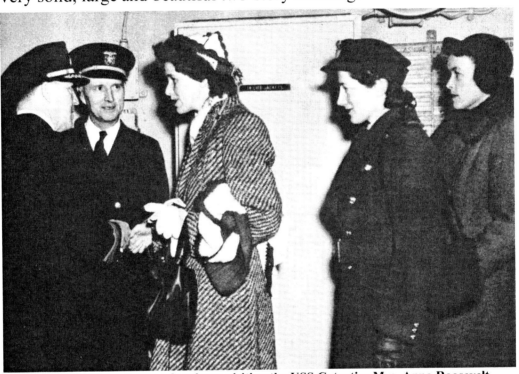

Figure 36. Three famous daughters visiting the USS Catoctin: Mrs. Anna Roosevelt Boettiger, Mrs. Sarah Churchill Oliver, and Miss. Kathleen Harriman. US Navy Photo.

While at Sevastopol, our guests stayed overnight in staterooms on the main deck of the ship. Each guest was assigned a sailor to personally help them, as needed. Louis Singer, a good friend of mine, was assigned to President Franklin Delano Roosevelt. In the early evening, Louis's buzzer rang and he quickly went to see what the President wanted. The President asked him if he could play gin rummy. When Louis told President Roosevelt that he could, the President told Louis to sit down and play gin rummy with him. He later told me what a great time he had playing cards with the President. I think he let the President win the card game!

Figure 37. The "Czar's Summer Palace" in Yalta, Crimea. Image from James Preuett.

While at Sevastopol, the Soviet Navy held an afternoon party for the U.S. Navy. This was held in a building, which was the only building left standing from the war attacks by the Germans. This building had no water or electricity, and the only beverage served was vodka. It was a very good party with entertainment and plenty of food.

We soon left for our return to our home base at Naples, Italy. And, just a few days later, we learned we were returning to the United States and docking at Philadelphia Navy Yard for a complete overhaul and a new paint job. After leaving Philadelphia, we traveled to San Diego, California for supplies and we then headed for Ulithi Atoll where many, many ships were congregating for the big push – the invasion of Japan.

A few days later, news came over our public address system that Japan had surrendered. This was truly a day to celebrate! We had a charting room on the ship, which was used only during invasions. However, during our free time, we used this area for playing cards or games. When this news came over the public address System, we decided we needed to celebrate. At this point, many who had smuggled an alcoholic beverage onboard the ship produced them.

We had our own private celebration at sea with 12 to 14 sailors gathered. Unfortunately, our beverage supply did not last long and our celebration took place during the afternoon hours, so we then had to wait for our evening meal. We were indeed a bunch of very happy sailors.

Now that our plans for going to Japan were changed, we then started landing troops in many cities in China, Korea, and Okinawa. We soon received orders to return to the U.S.A.

Our captain called his executive crew together and advised us that we could all be home for Christmas or we could go to Shanghai, China. It was decided to go to Shanghai where all the crew had a chance to visit and explore this city. Shanghai was divided in two sections – the old and the new – a very good R & R trip indeed!

We then left for our return trip to the United States, our captain pushed the ship to its top performance and we arrived in San Diego, California on December 12, 1945 in time for Christmas. I had to return to the ship, which was then at Norfolk, Virginia. After returning to the USS *Catoctin* for a few days, I was transferred to Great Lakes for discharge, which took place on January 16, 1946.

Overall, my naval experience provided me a very good two years of traveling almost three-quarters around the world, with few personal injuries, and enjoying my association with many, many others along the way. After arriving back to my home in Michigan, I returned to work at A & P Food Stores where I worked for 27 years. And later, I operated my own supermarket (a Spartan store) in Houghton Lake, Michigan. I am now happily retired and living in Traverse City, Michigan.

MEMORIES – NONE – ONLY NIGHTMARES
Albert N. Roberts
US Army, Detroit, Michigan

I was born in Detroit, Michigan. At age 22, I was drafted and told to report for duty for service to my country. My time served was from January 21, 1942 to October 25, 1945. My total service time was 3 years, 10 months, 5 days. I served in the 3rd Medical Battalion Company A. My military occupational specialty was Truck Driver Light #345.

My campaigns and battles were: North Apennines, Algeria, French Morocco, Tunisia, Sicily, Naples, Foggia, Rome, Arno, Southern France, Rhineland, and Central Europe.

Decorations and Citations received: Good Conduct Medal, Distinguished Unit Badge, European Service Medal, African Service Medal, Middle Eastern Service Medal, and eight (8) Bronze Stars.

I was at Fort Ord, California, for boot camp and headed to Africa on October 24, 1942. I was cocky and ready to fight!! Neither boot camp nor my time

Figure 38, Albert N. Roberts at Fort Ord, California.

in Africa prepared me for the beachhead landing in Normandy. On our way over in the boats, the seas were rough and most of us were sick either from the seas, nerves or lack of sleep.

When we reached the beachhead, we had to go ashore in Higgins Boats. Gun and mortar fire were continuous. As the front of the boat dropped, the men in front of me were killed instantly. I jumped over the side of the boat into cold water up to my neck. I pushed a dead body ahead of me in the surf to get to the beach. It was then I realized, "This is for real – This is war and I had just used a fellow American as a shield." That's when I began praying, "Let me get through this living hell and back home to the States." There were dead bodies everywhere and the water was red!

I marched across Europe seeing piles of dead bodies, the smell so bad it made you sick. I saw the total destruction of cities and towns. There were homeless people and little kids with no parents. You just pushed on, living one day at a time. You were always tired, nervous, and never clean. Most of my battalion was killed during the invasion.

We went weeks with no showers and then they would come out and pick up a truck load of GI's and take us back behind the lines. We would be de-loused, given a chance to take a shower and shave, get a hot meal, catch up on some sleep and then back to the fighting. It was when you came back clean that you realized how bad you smelled when you left. Within a couple of days you smelled like everyone else again.

While in Rome I was among hundreds of GI's who were baptized by the Pope. I never had religion but sure needed it to get through those days of "Hell." I never believed I would get out alive and now at age 89 years, I wonder why I'm still here??

Memories – NONE – Only nightmares. I brought home a revolver and ammo from a fallen German soldier. That was my memory of the war. We are referred to as the "Amazing Generation," and "The Greatest Generation," for our service to this country and all we went through. It was an honor to serve and this is a great country to live in.

After returning home in 1945, I got a job truck driving for Fred Sanders in Detroit, Michigan. I retired to Florida in 1982 at the age of 62. My wife, a daughter and a son have all passed away. I stayed in Florida until 1999, at which time I moved back to Michigan to be by my only surviving daughter. I now reside at the Village at Bay Ridge, Assisted Living. I have outlived most of my friends and family.

I've put the war out of my mind. I don't care to talk about it. We live in a great country and I'm proud to have served.
ONE NATION UNDER GOD.

JACK'S STORY

Helen Roster
Traverse City, Michigan

When my husband came home from prison camp in Germany he said, someday he would like to write a book about life in prison camp. But, he said probably a lot of other servicemen would write one. Before he could get around to doing this he had a major stroke and was unable to read, write, talk or work for the next seventeen years of his life. He passed away in 1977 from a major Cerebral Hemorrhage. Therefore I submit Jack's story as a tribute to him.

Medals:
- Air Medal with two Oak Leaf Clusters
- Purple Heart with two Oak Leaf Clusters
- European-African-Middle Eastern Theater Ribbon, three Stars
- Good Conduct Medal
- Unit Citation Badge
- Two Overseas Bars.

In 1942 John (Jack) N. Roster and I were living in Detroit, Michigan, with our two small children, Jackie d Jerry, after having moved from Flint, Michigan. He was employed at Continental Motors but in Flint he had been employed as a meat cutter for the A&P Grocery Store. I did not like living in Detroit as we were living in a 12-apartment building. The front door literally opened directly onto the sidewalk with just the sidewalk between the apartment building and Vernon Highway. There was no area what-so-ever for the children to play outdoors.

One Sunday we decided to visit my parents in Flint and while there, Dad a Mom took us for a ride in the country. I said "if I see a house for rent I am moving whether you want to or not." We came across a little white house set way back off the road with a large front yard. Checking on it, it belonged to a girl that I went to school with. Now, I had never lived in the country and this had no running water or any kind of indoor plumbing but it did have a basement with about three feet of the coldest and clearest water with the sump pump running constantly. I had to make sure the basement door was locked at all times. I was desperate about getting out of Detroit so I rented it and moved with Jackie age three and Jerry age two. There was no telephone and I didn't have a car but I still moved, and Jack was to move as soon as he could.

Being a city girl I was scared to death at night so I did all of my house work at night until I was too tired to stay awake. In a few weeks Jack moved back to Flint and went back to work for the A&P as a meat cutter.

Jack always had a love for airplanes and of course with a war going on he wanted to enlist. Everyone thought he was crazy since he had a small family but he felt it was his duty for them. So with Jackie and Jerry I moved back home with my parents so that I could work and Mom & Dad would be my baby sitters. Our daughter Jackie had beautiful, long curly hair and before Jack left for the Service, he told Jackie not to let anyone cut her hair. Anytime she would see someone pick up a pair of shears she would cover her hair and run and hide crying out "I'll tell my Daddy". Before he left for camp he told the children that he would be home for Christmas and I told him not to say that because he didn't know where he would be but he insisted that he would be home for Christmas. One night while I was sleeping I woke up with someone knocking on my bedroom window. Sleepy I asked who it was and he answered, "Who do you think it is," so I said "what do you want?" He then said "what you think I want and let me in." While he was home, whenever I would ask when he had to be back in camp he would change the subject. After Christmas he said he had to leave for camp and the next day I received a call from one of his buddies and when I said he was on his way back the buddy said "OK, that's all I want to know." AWOL!

My moving back home with my two children didn't set too well with my 16 year old sister because she felt that I would use her as a baby sitter and she wouldn't get all the attention she had been getting. It also made it more crowded since my Grandma Gebhardt (Mom's mother) also lived there sharing my sister's bedroom. This was a family of full-blooded German people. Grandma refused to learn to speak English because she felt we would have to learn to speak German in order to talk to her and in this manner we would learn a second language. It was crowded but we made it work.

I was able to get employment in a small office in the center of the factory where the tanks rolled off the final assembly line. One day I was given the chance to bring a pair of slacks to work and drive a tank out in the yard. Back then no one wore slacks to work; we all wore skirts and blouses or sweaters. Later I was transferred to Bldg. #85 where I spent my days typing routing sheets. It was very boring work. This is where I was working when I received the telegram that Jack was missing in action.

When I found out my brother Bob was stationed in England with the Ordinance Department and Jack in England with the Air Force, I wrote to each one giving them each other's address. Bob went to see Jack for a few days and they had such a good time that Bob was restricted to Jack's air base for a few days. The next time he went to see Jack he was waiting for the planes to come back from a mission over Germany when Jack's plane was the only one that did not return that day. This was really hard on Bob because he knew for three months that Jack was missing in action but he couldn't let me know.

When I got home from work on the 17th of November, 1944 my mother said to me, "You had better sit down as I have something to tell you," but instead she handed me "The" telegram because she was crying too hard to talk. The telegram was hand written when they are normally typed and should be handed to the person involved and no-one else. This really bothered me and made me wonder all night if someone could be so cruel as to think it was funny or a joke.

When I got to work the next morning I was telling this sweet older gentleman, Dick Oberlin, who had the desk directly behind me about the telegram and after several hours he said "Look, this doesn't sound right to me either so I will cover for you while you run downtown to the telegraph office and check on this. We really couldn't imagine anyone playing such a cruel trick on anyone but you never know. I did go and check and it was for real and was handed the original telegram, but no explanation. I never heard anymore for three months when I received another telegram from the Government stating that Jack was a prisoner of war after having been missing for three months hiding from the Gestapo. He had been shot down over German territory and had saved his life by using his parachute

Membership Certificate
This is to certify that

T. Sgt. John N. Roster

Is a member of the Caterpillar Club whose life was spared the ___ day of ___ 19__ because of an emergency parachute jump from an aircraft. This certificate is bestowed to the end that this safety medium in the art of flying may be furthered.

PRESENTED THROUGH

Switlik Parachute Co.

CATERPILLAR CLUB

Figure 39. Jack Roster's Caterpillar Certificate from Switlik Parachute Company.

and so became a member of The Caterpillar Club. To become a member you have to save your life by using your parachute.

After I received the telegram that Jack was missing in action my Dad said to me "We don't know if Jack will ever be back but we pray and hope he will come home" but in the meantime we can be more comfortable. Mom and dad's house had a very large attic so he had two bedrooms added up there, one for me and one for Jackie and Jerry. We could go upstairs in the evening and give mom and dad some privacy and quiet time. We were much more comfortable after that and even more so when Jack came home and we could move out on our own.

We later learned that when Jack started out on his final B-17 mission over Holly, near Berlin, he had 21 raids and two Nazi planes destroyed to his credit. Captured after eleven days of hiding, Jack was brutally tortured by the Gestapo for six and a half hours. During his captivity, Jack escaped six times, only to be recaptured each time. They beat and tortured him after every escape attempt. Finally, the German Army sentenced him to be shot at sunrise. That night, the Russians started a surprise attack and in the confusion of retreat the records were lost and he was able to escape to a British Army unit.

On his trip back to the States the meat cutter on board ship became ill and knowing that Jack had also been a meat cutter he was asked to fill in. When they arrived back in the States Jack was given two very large smoked hams which he carried home in his duffel bag. Since we were on meat rationing my mother and I were very happy since ham was and has been our favorite meat, and still is for me. He loved to tease my mother (even before he went into the Service) by sneaking up behind her and untying her apron strings while she was working at the kitchen sink and acting as if he didn't know what she was talking about when she would get after him. One day as she was peeling vegetables he really got upset and asked her what she was doing? She said "getting supper ready and he wanted to know what she was going to do with the peels?" She said of course, she was dumping them in the garbage and I thought he was going to have a stroke, having been so hungry in Germany. After his time in the Veteran's Hospital in Florida and getting a job at home he said to me "take my check and first buy groceries and then take care of other expenses next."

When he arrived back in Flint after his time spent in the German prisoner-of-war camps he was very nervous when I met him at the bus Station and he said "look, I don't want to hear one word of German or I won't be able to stick around the house. Now, I am a full blooded German and all of our relatives are also and of course they all wanted to see him and were there at the house when we came home from the bus station. Grandma Gebhardt spoke only German. My parents spoke a lot of German since they came to this country when they were nine and eleven years old. So they had to learn English the hard way in school just by listening. They had come from Siberia, Russia. My dad's step-mother (actually, the wicked witch that I think she was; the one that gave step-mothers such a bad name) was at the house when we got back from the bus station, among many German neighbors and of course she was trying to convince Jack that he got good treatment from the Germans. I could see that Jack was about to explode so I took mom aside and said I was going to take Jack out of there and go visit his brother Bud who was the only one of five brothers who wasn't in the service (which really bothered Bud) but it was because of an existing health problem.

I can't remember how long he was home before he had to report to the Coral Gables Veteran's Hospital in Coral Gables, Florida, for treatment on the injuries he received on his hard tree landing when he was shot down. While in the hospital at Coral Gables there was a gentleman called "Silver Dollar Jake" who would come to the hospital and take a group of veterans out to a nice restaurant and bar and treat them to a nice dinner and drinks and give each one a silver dollar to remember him by.

My mind is totally blank of when Jack was released from the Coral Gables Veteran's Hospital. It must have been that he was discharged from there. After he was home Dick Oberlin, my co-worker from Bldg. #85, gave us one of his cottages at Houghton Lake for a week to say "Thank You Jack" for your time in the Service.

After a period of time getting re-acquainted with his two children and resting, Jack went back to work for the A&P. We found a house to rent and eventually bought it and all was going well. Surprise, surprise when we found out we were expecting a new little one and our youngest at that time was Jerry who was fourteen-years old. This was a complete surprise and shocker because the doctors at the Veteran's Hospital told him he would probably be sterile because of the treatment he received in prison camp.

After our little boy Mark was born, Jack called me from the store and asked if I was going to the baby shower that night and when I said "yes" he said "don't get a baby sitter because I will come home early and bring pork chops and baby sit while you go to the shower". That was the last I heard from him for a week and we were going crazy trying to figure out where he was and why.

After a week had gone by I was awakened one night by a phone call from him and he sounded like he was very drunk. I asked him where he was and if he was coming home?" He said "I don't know, where is home?" My first thought was "Oh Lordy, is he ever drunk". So I told him to get into a cab and tell the driver to take you home to our address after repeating the address over and over. I told him just follow these instructions and I would pay the cabbie when he was delivered home.

I heard no more for over an hour (which seemed like an eternity) and was wondering "now what?" The cab finally did show up and I knew something was definitely wrong when I saw him and had such a hard time convincing him to go to bed because he said his head hurt so badly. After he was in bed for a short time he started shaking so hard that the bed was vibrating. The following morning I called my mother to let her know he was home, and asked her to come and see him explaining the condition he was in. She said he was probably trying to pull the wool over my eyes to cover up for having a good time while I was home with the kids and worrying so much. But, when she saw him she started to cry and said "Helen, this is no act" he needs help. I took him downtown on the bus to the Veteran's Office and couldn't get any help because we didn't have an appointment.

When I got home after many embarrassing moments on the bus, I called his bother and my sister's husband to see if they could help me. They decided we were going to the Dearborn Veteran's Hospital and there again they said they couldn't help me because we didn't have an appointment and to take him home and go through the proper channels. These two guys said "no way, he received this condition because of his time in the service and we were not taking him home and that they were going to take care of him. After spending about a week there he was sent home with the diagnosis of possible amnesia. I believe these events were actually his first mini-stroke. I later learned that his week away from home was spent staying in Chicago with his uncle and step-aunt where they said he walked up and down the alley all day. They thought he was having family problems and didn't want to call me for fear of interfering. After he came home from the Dearborn hospital he eventually went to work as a Foreman at the South Fisher Body Plant I in Flint, Michigan.

One evening while Jack was reading the newspaper, and he did read it from cover to cover, especially the want-ads, he saw an ad for a house with two cottages advertised for sale on Big Platte Lake in Honor, Michigan. He called about the ad and the next day the realtor from Beulah, Michigan, was in our house in Flint. He was some salesman and within two weeks we were the new proud owners of property on Big Platte Lake but the problem was Jack didn't have a job now. So, the answer to that (according to the realtor) was to buy a small business which we did and we eventually lost the business, because Jack was too good at giving out credit to people who didn't pay their bills. We had a great place on Big Platte Lake but Jack didn't have any employment. He did find a job again as a meat cutter but in Wyoming, Michigan, and roomed with a co-worker and came home up North on week-ends.

Six years after the birth of our second son, Mark, we got the news of another pregnancy and when this son, Jack. Jr.-Nick, was six months old I received a phone call from Grand Rapids stating that my husband had suffered a stroke and so my son-in-law Ron rushed me to St. Mary's Hospital in Grand Rapids. The nuns had been taking good care of him and when the Mother Superior came into his room to check on him, she looked at his tray and he had his back to it and couldn't turn by himself because he was completely paralyzed on his right side. She helped him turn and then whipped his tray away and said he needed good food, not what had been brought to him. With the paralysis he also lost his speech. After a week in the hospital we were told he could go home.

At this time I was working in the Rehabilitation Department at Munson Medical Hospital and Dr. Sladek was head of the Rehabilitation Department. When he heard about Jack he went to work to get him in the Speech Department at Dearborn's Veteran's Hospital. He was the first patient from this area to go to that facility. He improved to the point where he could walk and do most everything but his right hand never came back to normal nor did he ever recover his speech. He could only say about five words and if he did learn a new word, he would lose an old one. The one word he never did lose was "COFFEE', so we spent 17 years playing guessing games and charades. When he clapped his hands with one hand on top of the other this meant he wanted a sandwich.

When I first went to work after he had his big stroke it was as a Key Punch Operator on the midnight shift in Traverse City, and I was living in Honor at Big Platte Lake. I would get home about 9 AM and would be very tired since I still had to keep up our home and the cottages and would be dying for a few hours of sleep. He would want me to sit at the kitchen table and would say "what, what?" I know he wanted to know what had happened during the night but nothing went on except key punching with three 15 minute breaks during the night and no talking while working. After guessing for many minutes, I would say to Jack "can't you just try to write one word for me and then maybe I could guess what you want?" My little Nick was still so young and small that his little nose just came to the table top and always stood there while we were playing charades and said very seriously one morning can't you just write one word for me Daddy so I could guess?"

When Nick was 17 years old he was going to high school in Traverse City because had we moved to make it easier for me to work. We were living on Tibbets Lake and Nick had gone to a Christmas party at the high school while I was finishing shortening a pair of trousers for Jack to wear to a Christmas party. I was in the lower level where I had my sewing room and Jack came to the top of the stairs to let me know he wanted a sandwich by clapping his hands and saying "coffee". I took care of him and went to bed because I had to work the next day. I was rudely awakened by Nick almost tearing my bedroom door off the wall. He was all excited and scared because he couldn't wake up his father who was slumped over sideways in his lounge chair with a warm cup of coffee sitting on his end table and a cigarette burn the full length of the cigarette in the carpeting.

Nick called the East Bay Volunteer Fire Department and Nick was still holding the phone in his hand when the volunteers came bursting into the house. They went to work fast and Jack was rushed to Munson Hospital but he never regained consciousness and passed away two days later on December 23rd, 1977. His death was caused by a massive cerebral hemorrhage. Sadly, my birthday is on December 25th, Christmas Day, and the funeral was held on December 26th, 1977.

Figure 40. Tank Commander Benjamin Russell, Korea 1951.

Figure 42. MM2 Benjamin Russell, USS *Seawolf* (SS-197), Pacific, 1944.

Figure 41. Lucille and Benjamin Russell, wedding in 1952

A Gut Feeling He Couldn't Shake

Lucille Russell
Hart, Michigan

After witnessing the Pearl Harbor attack in 1941, Benjamin
Russell and his brother Scott joined the United States Navy in
December of that year and both wanted to serve on submarines. They
spent five days/weeks in boot camp at the Great Lakes Naval Center
where they performed some tests to confirm whether they were
submariner "worthy." One test they experienced was holding their
breath. They were instructed to hold their breath for two minutes
while holding a mirror under their nose. The mirror was used to
ensure they did not breathe out. Ben expelled all his breath and held it,
slowly breathing air into his lungs rather than out. Since he was
breathing in, he didn't' steam the mirror – so he passed!

After Scott and Ben finished testing, they transferred directly to
Pearl Harbor, skipping over submarine school. Both Ben and his
brother Scott went on to Australia and were assigned to the 61st Relief
Crew and assigned to the submarine tender USS *Holland* (AS-3), out
of Albany, West Australia. From there they transferred north to
Freemantle where they were assigned to the *Tambor*-class submarine,
USS *Thresher* (SS-200).

After duty aboard the *Thresher*, Ben was assigned to the USS
Seawolf (SS-197), and made three war patrols. One fateful day they
were docked at Pearl Harbor and getting ready to go underway for her
15th war patrol when Ben had a gut feeling he couldn't shake. Just
before they pulled from the dock something drove him to find the
skipper, Lieutenant Commander Bontier. When he found him, Ben
told him he did not like him or the crew and wanted off the *Seawolf*.
The captain told him to get off the submarine. Not surprising, since
submariners must get along working in such close quarters. Ben leapt
from the sub as it was pulling away and no one ever saw the *Seawolf*
again. She was sunk on that patrol with all hands lost.

Ben was also assigned to the USS *Plunger* (SS-179) based at
Midway and lastly, he was stationed on the USS *Sea Cat* (SS 399), as

a Machinist Mate 2nd Class. Ben served on the USS *Sea Cat* until the end of WWII. The *Sea Cat* earned three battle stars for her services during the Second World War. Benjamin Russell was honorably discharged on October 1, 1945.

Ben and Scott reminisced often and relayed their stories to friends and family. I recall one story in particular about the pranks they played on new shipmates assigned to their submarine. One fellow was intentionally and incorrectly instructed on how to flush the head (toilet). There were certain valves and various positioning of the valves relayed to the young man. The young man listened intently and took note of the false instructions. When the time came to test the instructions the result was, let's say, in his face.

Another occasion of toilet disasters was when an anonymous crewmember turned the wrong valves and all the toilets shot water through the air conditioning system. The toilet water sprayed throughout the submarine and even in the officers' quarters where they were reviewing maps and making plans. As you can imagine, they were not pleased about the mishap. They never found out who did it and they had to surface to clean up the mess.

During one Christmas holiday, Ben and his shipmates experienced a relentless depth charging. Their cook had a turkey in the oven for the holiday meal, but every time a depth charge would detonate, the turkey would shoot out of the oven like out of a cannon. Exasperated, the cook would put the turkey back in the oven. Nevertheless, to his consternation, it would come right back out over and over again. In the end, the cook was so exhausted from the ordeal he just threw the turkey away.

While in port, Ben and his shipmates were partaking in some 'good cheer' and spirits were high. Upon returning to the sub, Ben wanted to bring his camera onboard. The guard on duty stopped them and explained that cameras were not allowed on the ship and sent them away. Ben and his mates were a bit inebriated and didn't want to part with the camera and fond memories captured within so they decided to hide the camera outside of the gate. Ben figured that when they docked again they could find the camera for their next liberty call. Well, the day came for liberty and when they searched out the camera, they could not find it. Calling off the search for the camera, Ben and his mates went to the local pub and partook in merriment once again. They decided to look for the camera again and this time, with the help of their inebriated state they were able to find it immediately!

Ben joined the Army on March 14, 1949. He was stationed in Japan when the Korean War broke out. He was assigned to the 25th Tank Division and the 89th Tank Battalion. He was a Tank Commander for the "Always Able" Company, duly named for their outstanding service on the Korea front. Front line duty record of the Always Able Company was the highest at 200 days on the battle line with only an eight day rest. Ben and his gang joked that those eight days weren't' rest, they were days spent lubricating and repairing the tanks.

Ben always joked that cigarettes saved his life and told the story about one evening on guard duty. He was sitting by the tank on guard while the other soldiers were sleeping and decided to have a cigarette. He wore a hooded raincoat and stooped down under the hood to light it. Any light may indicate their location to enemy snipers so he was always cautious of that fact. As he bent to light the cigarette, he heard a bullet zing by his head and hit the tank. A sniper had him in his sight all along but Ben had avoided the bullet by bending down to light up.

He came home on leave in May 1952 and met Lucille Cummins and they were soon married. Ben and Lucille were stationed in California at Camp Cook until November when they sent him to Fort Lewis, Washington. From there they were transferred to Germany.

All together Ben was on eight submarine patrols and earned a Presidential Unit Citation and Four Battle Stars while in the US Navy. Later, as a Master Sergeant in the US Army, Ben received his second Presidential Unit Citation for heroic work performed early in the Korean War, specifically for the battle of Masan. We lived in the Detroit area as Ben taught at Detroit Arsenal in Warren, Michigan until his 20 year retirement from the military. Ben was a proud member of the Hart American Legion Post 234, the Hart VFW and

US SubVets, WWII. After his military retirement, Ben started Russell's Ridge Ski Resort in Elbridge Township in Oceana County. He also owned and operated Russell Construction until his retirement. All of this, with Lucille by his side; Ben and Lucille were blessed with two sons and three daughters and their spouses, along with several grandchildren and great-grandchildren.

UNITED STATES SUBMARINES LOST IN WORLD WAR II

**We remember with honor those who served
on the submarines known by the Russell Brothers**
*Grunion ✰ Grampus ✰ Grenadier
Grayling ✰ Wahoo ✰ Grayback
Trout ✰ Gudgeon ✰ Seawolf
Tang ✰ Escolar ✰ Kete ✰ Snook*

**There is a port of no return, where ships
May ride at anchor for a little space
And then, some starless night, the cable slips,
Leaving an eddy at the mooring place...
Gulls, veer no longer. Sailor, rest your oar.
No tangled wreckage will be washed ashore.**

"Lost Harbor" by Leslie Nelson Jennings

Ben Russell continued in service to this country during the Korean War. Letters home can show the emotions of thoughts during war assignments. I enclose the contents of letters sent home to his mother during his time in Korea.

In a letter dated March, 8 1951 Ben wrote...
Dear Mom: Well, here it is evening and tomorrow morning at 0430 we attempt to cross the Han River. We're only a few hundred feet from it now. That may be

rough; the Captain says if we make it the whole retriever crew will be decorated. I only hope it ain't daisy's I'm decorated with. As a rule, the retriever doesn't go with the lead tanks, but I guess this time being ours. The river is about 5 feet deep. We are supposed to be ready to use our winch and pull them out if they get stuck." I sent the $55 dollars, put it in the bank and how about the pictures I wanted you to send. Kinda' laying down on the job aren't you. Well if we get across here it will soon be over I guess. About April I might be out of here. Write often. Love, Ben

Another letter dated March 5, 1951 said:

Dear Mom: Well, your probably wondering most likely from my last note if I'm still alive, "I am" though I wonder how. Man they laid the heavy stuff on us we were with the lead tank, got it across safe but had to tow one that got "swamped." A Colonel from the 35th Regiment, 25th Division said it was the "prettiest job he ever seen done." It sure took a lot of willpower to crawl out of that retrieve and hook up the cables and such; and to top it off, the cable broke and we had to get out and repair it and all the time this artillery and mortar is screaming and busting all around. None of our crew got hurt except me. A lot of Infantry got it though and they sure were trying to stop us from crossing. Well, I've gotta get some sleep and so forth. It's a lovely, muddy day here; warm and sunny though. I'll write and let you know if I get the Congressional Medal of Honor, but I'll probably get busted instead. With love, Ben. P. S. – Their sure laying it into them today too, but our work is done, unless something happens.

Figure 43. USS *Seawolf* (SS-197) as she is launched during her commissioning ceremonies at Portsmouth Naval Shipyard, Kittery, ME. US Navy Photograph, in the public domain

THE NAVY DOCTOR
Susan Sayre
Detroit, Michigan

This is a little family story; I want to tell to my children, grandchildren and great-grandchildren about your family history during the era of WWII and following. I, your mother Susan, was one of four children; three sisters and one brother. Your dad, George, was one of three siblings; two brothers and one sister. Your father and I were married on December 21, 1940. As you learned in history, World War II was being fought in Europe and on December 7, 1941 Pearl Harbor was attacked and our involvement in the war began. Being a physician, your father was very soon involved. He signed up for Navy duty, obtained his uniforms and soon was leaving for duty assignment out of Alameda, California. After arranging to store our furniture, your father and I traveled by train on a five-day journey. He was "pretty sure" he would be back home with his family in six months.

I was pregnant, due in January of 1942, so I came back from California after saying goodbye to your Dad. I lived for a time with my parents and for a time with dad's parents. Occasionally, Frank and I would travel to St. Claire, Michigan to visit my dear, dear grandmother, Mary Gliem, and stay there for a week or two. I didn't know "beans with the bag open" about a new baby so it was great to have parents and grandparents around for guidance and assistance.

Figure 44. Lieutenant George Sayre, USN

Dad was the doctor on a converted United Fruit Company boat, SS *La Perla*, which was later commissioned by the US Navy as the cargo ship US *Cygnus*, (AF-23). His ship was a refrigerated boat and supplied food for the troops on the islands of the South Pacific, their home port being Auckland, New Zealand. Dad's tour of duty continued for much longer than six months. It was later determined that his orders for discharge had gone down with a crashed plane and nobody knew to do anything about that.

While dad was away, I made use of my time by doing volunteer work. I was involved with the American Women's Voluntary Services where I worked as a hostess for dignitaries, greeting them when they came to town and driving them to the factories as needed. I volunteered in many other areas, often arranged by my mother in law, who was also my babysitter for Frank. She was strong-medicine and I learned a lot from her about strength as a woman. By living with my

Figure 45. Lieutenant George Sayre.

parents, Frank bonded strongly with his grandfather, eventually becoming a dentist, as his grandfather was.

Dad returned home to the States in 36 months, which, as mentioned before, was a much longer tour away from his family than we had planned; only he *did* return; for many men of his age did not return from their service. For this merciful blessing I was eternally grateful. And, of course you are, too; for you all are fortunate siblings of a good father, a fine role model and a man who lived proud being your father.

After the war ended, he had many points that helped him to be discharged among the first to come home. His last assignment was to the Navy's Great Lakes Station in

Wisconsin. While there he met Dr. Bradley Harris, who had tentative plans to go back to the University of Michigan for a surgical residency. Dr. Harris had a family practice in Ypsilanti which he offered to your father so that it would be kept open and care would continue for his patients. By accepting Dr. Harris's offer, dad would have an office in which to establish his private medical practice. This opportunity gave us a reason to settle in Ypsilanti, Michigan. Eventually your dad returned to the University of Michigan to specialize in OB Gynecology and opened an individualized, single practice. For a time, I worked as the secretary in this office.

Frank was two years old when his father came home from his Navy duty. The rest of the siblings births were Jane in 1946, George Jr. in 1948 and Elizabeth in 1951.

Our starter home was a two bedroom on Stanley Street in Ypsilanti, Michigan. As your dad's practice grew and became better established, we could better afford a larger home. He

Figure 46. Susan and Dr. George Sayre.

found a four bedroom home at 1208 Whittier Street, Ypsilanti, Michigan. We moved to this home that year and the boys shared a bedroom and the girls, Jane and Elizabeth, shared another.

Your father died in 1996 and I still have an incredible longing for the strong man with whom I shared my life. I have to say that while your father and I had a great life filled with success and good favor, I am most proud of all of you and your children. Together we tried to model good work ethics and values, strong character, good role modeling, pride for hard work and also tried to instill a sense of humor in your lives. How could I feel anything but pride: Frank becoming a dentist, following in your grandfather's footsteps; Jane as a Librarian at the University of Michigan's Library of Sciences; George Jr. also as a dentist following both his grandfather and older brother; and Elizabeth with your degree in Secondary Education and working as a Management Consultant. All of you combined are the sum of my greatest accomplishments.

Editor's Note: Notes from the Ann Arbor District Library regarding Mayors of Ypsilanti state that:

> *Susan Sayre with four growing youngsters was drawn into City and school activities to which she brought intelligence and enthusiasm. Through the League of Women Voters, she became aware of the need of the City for a new hospital, she assisted with a 20 year effort and the new, state of the art Beyer Memorial Hospital was begun in 1967. Susan served on the City Council from 1962 to 1968 and was elected Mayor of Ypsilanti in 1968. She was instrumental in founding the famous, outdoor Greek Theater opened at Briggs Stadium on the campus of Eastern Michigan University; hiring Burt Larr to appear in the comedy "The Birds": and Dame Judith Anderson to star in the tragedies. During her time as Mayor, the City Water Purification Plant on old Race Street near Spring Street was enlarged and the Old Ladies' Library was moved from 130 N. Huron Street to the remodeled Post Office building on W. Michigan and it became the Ypsilanti Public Library. It is notable that Susan Sayre was the first woman elected as the Mayor of Ypsilanti.*

GOLD STARS

Virginia Smith
Honor, Michigan

The airwaves were filled with news about WWII. Patriotic songs filled the air. Citizens of our free nation were working together to support the war, the cause for freedom. Our small town was touched by the sacrifices of war, just like many other communities. I was a young girl in high school; could I understand the emotional impact of the war? Well, I probably could not, but I sure felt like I could!

I would walk along the streets of town and see stars in the windows. During the war, stars in the windows told a story of the men serving in the war and the homes touched by their service. I learned that a blue star hanging in a window meant that a person from that home was in the military service and away from home. While the absence of a family member seemed like a sad thing to me, I quickly learned that a blue star was a good thing. It gave the message that that family was committed to a cause bigger than their own needs. The fact that it was blue also gave the message that that service member was alive.

I remember a day when my mother and other women in the community came together to help out at one of these decorated homes. But, it turned out that the star hanging in the window was no longer blue, it was now gold. When a blue star turned to gold it meant that that serviceman had died in the war. Usually a telegram was delivered by military personnel, announcing the death and confirming that that serviceman would not be returning to his family. That gold star told the community that one of our own had sacrificed their life for our freedom. I could see the pain in the women's eyes as they comforted each other.

Even as a young girl, I could feel that pain, my heart would ache and I would be brought to tears. Two young men in our school left to go to war at a very young age. They earned their graduation certificate but they were not present for the ceremony; duty called and they were gone. Their mamas hung blue stars in their windows in "honor" of their sons, in a small town called Honor. And, we all prayed that their stars would stay blue. Many did and many did not.

I would listen to the radio waiting for news and also hoping for the reprieve provided by entertainment. I found that even the songs that were sung spoke to our nation about the effects of war on families. The popular singer Tex Ritter would sing, "There's A Gold Star In Her Window." This song would move me to tears as I ached for the mothers as they grieved, yet also feeling pride for the accomplishments of her loved son or daughter.

I graduated from Honor Rural Agricultural High School in 1944. I later met and married John Thomas Smith, a US Navy Veteran. Living through that time in America instilled an incredible patriotism in me. I am moved to tears by patriotic songs and stories of the sacrifices of war. I pray for the young men and women today that unselfishly take a pledge to defend our freedoms and put their lives in harm's way. We no longer place blue stars in our windows but the sacrifice of missing a loved one gone off to war is the same as it always has been.

Figure 47. Mrs. Virginia and John Thomas Smith. Photo from Virginia Smith.

To this day, whenever I hear that song or read the words, my eyes well with tears and my heart aches for all of those who lost a loved one in War. When I hear this song I am transported back to the time when I was the young teenager, feeling the sad memories and learning about life, in a small town in America. I present the words of the song that helped shape me into the woman I am today; a proud and patriotic American. God Bless America.

There's A Gold Star In Her Window

Words and Music by Tex Ritter and Frank Harford

There's a little gray-haired lady
You know as well as I,
Her eyes are always smiling
When yours and mine would cry.
Tho' she seems almost happy,
Her thoughts are far away;
She knows her boy is waiting
Where she will go someday.

There's a gold star in her window,
Shining bright and clear for all the world to see.
There's a gold star in her window,
Of the part a mother plays to keep us free.
To aid the cause of Liberty
She proudly gave a son.
Without the deeds of men like he,
No war is ever won.

There's a gold star in her window,
For a lad who led the way to victory.
There's a gold star in her window,
Shining bright and clear for all the world to see.
There's a gold star in her window,
Of the part a mother plays to keep us free.

'Twill shine throughout eternity
To guide us on our way.
Lest we forget or fail to see
The part we have to play.
There's a gold star in her window,
For a lad who led the way to victory.

Figure 48. A "Sons in Service" flag from WWII era

The family "Sons in Service" flags were usually about a foot long and were hung vertically in a window. The flags were common in WWI and II to designate a family member in the service (blue stars) or having died in action (gold star overlaying the blue). Corporations and institutions also used them to denote the service of employees and members. Their use remains authorized by Congress.

A FOUR-MONTH ODYSSEY
Dorothy Stiegmeyer
Cincinnati, Ohio

In early 1944, the US Government decided that there could be no more deferments for young men under 26 and it appeared that my husband Ken would be inducted into the service. He thought that he would be eligible to get a commission in the Navy so he went to the Navy recruiter and applied. Unfortunately he had difficulty with his eye sight so he came home and we ate carrots for a month. When he returned a month later to the recruitment center, his eye sight had not improved. This meant he would soon be drafted.

On the day of departure, he had a badly infected tooth, so there was a reprieve. After three years of marriage, we were expecting a child near the end of June. When the next call came, our baby was due any day, so Ken was given a one month deferment. Our son, John, was born July 1, 1944. In those days, hands-on baby care by fathers was very rare. But Ken enjoyed sharing John's care, including diapering.

The day finally came, on August 1, 1944, that our brand new family had to be split apart and Ken was sent to Camp

Figure 49. Dorothy Stiegmeyer and her son John. Photo from Dorothy Stiegmeyer.

Fannin, a US Army training facility, and POW camp, near Tyler, Texas, for basic training in the infantry. Right from the start his letters described a pretty arduous physical routine. It was a far cry from desk work at General Motors and most of his letters spoke of how much he missed his family.

In September, my parents came to Michigan to take John and I to Boston. Ken's letters were full of longing for us to be with him in Texas. There were other service wives in his company and he assured us it would be easy for us to find a home to start with. Needless to say, my loving parents were reluctant to send their firstborn grandson 2,000 miles away. We had to have a train reservation and the trip was not a one day trip. My dad, pulling a few strings, was able to get a Pullman reservation to a town near Tyler. We all worked to plan what one would need to care for a three month old. Imagine all the diapers and also a container to put all the dirty diapers in. We decided to use a streamer trunk for all the diapers and clothes. We shipped a carriage and a swing. I took the overnight train to Indianapolis. After leaving the depot in Boston, the conductor unfortunately discovered that three people had the same upper berth; a businessman, a military man, and John and I and we all had reservations and tickets stating so. God Bless the military man who gave up his right to the berth. I don't recall what happened to the businessman but we ended up in the berth.

In Indianapolis, we transferred to a club car where John screamed all the way to St. Louis. Ken's Uncle Fred met us there. He was waiting right there for the two of us when we got off the train. Once we were in his loving arms, the screaming stopped and there was a wonderful smile from both mother and baby. The following day was a day of washing diapers and clothes, rest and enjoyment with Ken's relatives. One of Ken's aunts was astounded with all that was involved in bringing a three month old half way across the country and that we included John's favorite stuffed animal which was a giraffe, not cuddly but big.

On day three we took off for Texas, arriving in the early afternoon. Ken, being a buck private could not meet us, so he sent the wife of an Army buddy to help us from the train to the bus, which took us to Tyler. She was from Ken's hometown and was very nice, although I had never met her.

So, the news was that Ken was unable to find a temporary home for us. Off we went to the USO. The story there was that there was no place available. I thought that we would have to go to a hotel. Mary was watching John while I went to the restroom. Two young wives of a lieutenant and a sergeant came looking for someone with a baby who needed a home. Their landlady had sent them because she had a room available. She felt it was more difficult for a young woman with a baby to find a place to stay and she loved children. How thankful we were for having the USO, being a place to go for help and all the wonderful people who were willing to share their homes with young families.

What a household it was. It was a brand new colonial style with large rooms. There was no washing machine or vacuum cleaner. From five in the morning until midnight the kitchen was always full of activity. Two busy mothers needed to sterilize bottles, four families were preparing food, and Mrs. Rogers baked something every day. She baked bread, biscuits, cakes pies and preparing chitins. We washed the sheets, diapers, and towels in the bathtub with a plunger and our clothes in the kitchen sink.

When Ken had free nights, we would walk to the bus station to greet him, and walk back and then sit on the stool in the bathroom to visit with him while he soaked in the tub. He didn't' always get to stay the night. So on other nights, Mrs. Rogers would watch John while I took the bus to Camp Fannin. She would rock John and sing folksy spiritual songs. On Sundays, when Ken was free, we took the street car, and then walked to the Lutheran church for services. When Ken was on duty, John and I went to the Baptist church nearby with Mrs. Rogers. What a contrast between the two styles of worship.

On Thanksgiving, I prepared a full Thanksgiving dinner; pumpkin pie and all. John and I were all alone in the house which was usually so full of life. Late in the afternoon I found out that Ken couldn't get off base. There were lots of falling tears, but in came Bill, the lieutenant, with his family. They just had dinner at the Officer's Club, but he sat down and ate dinner with John and I.

Come Christmas, the Rogers were going away so Mrs. Rogers showed me their Christmas gift to us, a live chicken. I told her it was very thoughtful but I would not be able to kill it or clean it. The dear woman killed it and cleaned it for us. What a joy she was. Her singing, her laughter, and her encouragement never seemed to waiver.

The times in Tyler were the best of times and the worst of times. Because of the Battle of the Bulge, the soldiers were being shipped without leave. These were months when you knew what was important in life. It was a mixture of joy, sorrow and fear. There was so much compassion and helpfulness. We didn't have the amenities that we were used to. We didn't take others for granted. We treasured the time we had together.

Ken had been selected to go to Georgia to Officers Training School. At the end of January, Ken left for Georgia and we had to say good-bye to those who had nurtured us and shared our lives for the last four months. It was a most adventurous journey, a time when I learned a new way of life and love with people who I learned to care for dearly.

LOVE, WAR, AND HONOR
Mary Sykora
Berwyn, Illinois

This is a story of love, war, and honor. It is a story about Captain Lawrence J. Sykora, MD and his wife Mary whose love for each other and for country survived WWII. They are my parents and I, their daughter Dee, was born while my father was overseas.

My parents, both of Czechoslovakian decent, were born in 1917 and were children of the depression. They met in college and fell in love. They married in 1939 and they began a life of promise. My father entered medical school and my mother took a job with Sears and Roebuck in Chicago. When my father was accepted to King's Hospital in Brooklyn, New York for his internship, Sears transferred my mother there also. They lived in a dark basement apartment where my mother could see the legs of the people walking

Figure 50. Lawrence and Mary Sykora

by and little else. Every day, she would take the subway into New York to work while my father spent many hours at the hospital, sometimes sleeping there. He had just finished his internship when the Japanese bombed Pearl Harbor and the United States could no longer ignore the chaos that was threatening freedom across the sea. America was now at war.

The military needed doctors and few doctors were spared because of age or marital status. Mom and dad's journey into the war had begun. Wherever dad went, my mother went too. He was drafted into Company B of the 319th Medical Battalion of the 94th Division and given the rank of Captain. On September 15th, 1942 the 94th

Infantry Division was activated. The place was Fort Custer, near Battle Creek, Michigan. The Commanding General of the 94th Infantry Division was Major General Harry J. Malony. Soon after activation, however, it was decided that the facilities at Fort Custer were inadequate and the 94th was moved in November to Camp Phillips, Kansas which was a theater of operations type camp. One story barracks were built of wood and tar. The campsite was bleak and windswept and fairly depressing. Three days after Christmas basic training began. The extremes in weather on the Kansas plains ranged

from sub-zero weather to rain and glue-like mud to oppressive heat and dust storms. On some occasions it became necessary to issue respirators and goggles to the guards to enable them to continue walking their posts.

In August of 1943, the division by motor moved to Camp Forrest in Tullahoma, Tennessee. There, the troops remained temporarily before arriving at Camp McClain, Mississippi in late November where the same wood and tar-paper barracks awaited them but the weather and terrain was a welcome relief from the windswept, treeless prairies where it was said, "there is nothing between us and Canada but barbed wire fences."

On May 5, 1944, the 94th Division was alerted for overseas duty. It was time for my parents to say good-

Figure 51. Captain Lawrence J. Sykora, MD, US Army. Photo provided by Mary Sykora

bye. They had my brother, Larry, by then who was 22 months old and my mother was pregnant with me. The troops boarded a train for New York and my mother and brother got into their old car in which she had placed a mattress in the back seat for him to sleep on and they began the journey back to Chicago where they would live with my

Grandparents. The road that my mother traveled paralleled the train tracks and Mom watched with a heavy heart as the train full of troops pulled out of the station. One of my father's buddies saw her car and told Dad to look out the window. He saw her, tears slipping from his eyes. She could not see him through the train windows but hoped that he would. She also was crying. Two lovers torn apart by war, one facing the horrors to come and possible death, the other the horror of worry and the feelings

Figure 52. Captain Lawrence Sykora and his wife Mary Sykora. Photo from Mary Sykora

of the unknown. I believe that the pit in my mother's stomach was bigger by far than the child growing inside of her and the little toddler in the old fashioned car seat next to her combined. My mother had to drive from Mississippi back to Chicago with her ration coupons for food, gas and tires. On the way, one of her tires went flat along a lonely stretch of road. Thankfully a wonderful gentleman stopped and put her spare tire on for her. He told her a little town was up the road a way and there she could find a man that would fix her tire. The town was just a few buildings long and she found the garage. The man that owned it gladly and for free fixed her flat tire by putting an old shoe in it. He told her that her spare would hold and that if any other tire went flat, the tire with the shoe would do until she got to Illinois. The tires made it and she arrived tired and sad but strong and brave as is her way.

In New York, the *Queen Mary* set sail with thousands of troops on her. She was escorted by aerial support for the first few miles and then she was on her own across the Atlantic. The 94th did themselves proud with only a few who "fed the fishes" mostly due to the heat and extremely crowded conditions on the ship. After sailing up the Clyde of Firth to Greenock, Scotland, the troops of the 94th began debarking the morning of August 12. The total debarking of all the troops on board was completed on August 13, 1944 where the Division moved to temporary stations in Wiltshire County in Southern England. As soon as the 94th arrived they began making preparations for entry into the combat zone. On August 30, 1944, the division was alerted that it would be moving to the continent. They boarded motor transport and were taken to Southampton, Weymouth and Portland where they boarded Liberty ships and other craft to cross the English Channel. From which port my father sailed I do not know but I can guess the tension was escalating tremendously as was the valor and dedication of the troops.

My father, Captain Sykora, was the Commander of Company B. His company was just behind the front fighting line and responsible for treating and saving our wounded soldiers. Behind Company B were the necessary support teams. During one battle with the Germans our front line was being pushed back and called for air support. Soon a single engine fighter-bomber flew over Company B and headed directly for the Germans. Dad and his medics could hear the bombs and gunfire which pushed the Germans back. Shortly afterward, they heard the plane returning. Sputtering and belching with smoke pouring out. It came down in a field just in front of dad and his men. Dad pulled the 19 year old Major from the plane and asked him how he felt. Shaken but not too badly hurt all the young major could say was, "Doc, are there any Krauts here? I've never seen one!" Dad was impressed with his exuberance but replied in the negative. Before sending him back to his air base he gave him a thorough examination and declared him fit.

During this time my mother was living with her parents. Dad's official address was that of his parents living nearby. One day two men knocked on his mother's door and gave her a registered letter from the Army. A shock wave rode over my grandparents but they did not open the letter. That evening they took the letter over to my other grandparents' house where mom was living. Mom was in the kitchen and could hear the four of them whispering to each other. They believed the letter contained the ultimate bad news and were trying to decide what to do. My mother, curious about their huddle, came into the room and asked what they were whispering about. They handed her the letter. Gripped by terrorizing fear she slowly opened it tears already beginning to well up in her eyes. After all, he had been in the thick on the fighting especially during the Battle of the Bulge and communications between them had been difficult. All she had was a scrap book in which she put every news clipping she could find about the 94th and the maps showing the advances of the US and Allied Troops. The letter said:

AWARD OF THE BRONZE STAR
MEDAL

Captain Lawrence J. Sykora, 0420510, Medical Corps, United States Army for meritorious service in connection with military operations against an enemy of the United States in France from 12 September 1944 to 29 January 1945. Captain Sykora assumed command of his medical company for four months prior to the day it was committed in combat. During this period, he made a diligent study to learn the particular attitudes, personalities and special training of his men and made necessary adjustment to form a well balanced and efficient team. Personally supervising the activities of his unit under fire, he frequently visited the advance aid stations solving critical evacuation problems on the spot. The superior leadership, untiring devotion to duty, and high sense of responsibility displayed by Captain Sykora were an inspiration to all concerned and reflect the highest credit upon himself and the Medical Corps.

-AND-

AWARD OF THE BRONZE STAR
MEDAL
(OAK LEAF CLUSTER)

Captain Lawrence J. Sykora, 0420510, Medical Corps, Company B, 319th Medical Battalion, United States Army, for meritorious achievement in connections with military operations against an enemy of the United States in Germany on 23 February, 1945. While returning from front line positions with an ambulance loaded with wounded soldiers, Captain Sykora noticed a wounded officer lying in the road. Unhesitantly going to his side and amid heavy artillery and mortar fire, he rendered first aid and directed his evacuation to the aid station. His deep concern for the welfare of others reflects great credit upon himself and the military service.

Needless to say, my mother still crying was now crying tears of joy and gratitude and immense love for my father. The recommendation for the Bronze Star Medal came from Lt. M. A. Surreall, MC commanding. In his recommendation he noted that my father had made it a point to know each man in his company personally and by name. He studied each man and by moving individuals about under his command was able to bring about and present a superior organization which was ready for combat shortly after he assumed command. After being committed to action, Captain Sykora personally directed all the activities of his company and by his constant devotion to duty and by his untiring efforts he has provided Combat Team 302 with medical support that has been exceptionally outstanding. Captain Sykora leads his men by his personable example. His outstanding success in handling men is due to the fact that he is firm and fair at he same time and that by his genuine interest in his men they have placed much confidence in him. Captain Sykora's loyalty to his organization and his devotion to his mission are exceptionally high. This determined though modest and unassuming officer has been an inspiration to all those who have served with him. His tenacity of purpose, his intense desire to accomplish the mission in the best possible manner and the inspiration he gives his men by his exemplary attitude are in accord with the highest Army tradition.

I was born April 10, 1945. My dad was still in Europe. It took a while for him to be notified. When the news came that mother was all right and he had a baby girl, he breathed a sigh of relief. On night in camp he decided to write me a letter that my mother would later give to me on my fortieth birthday. It was a letter of intense love and yearning. He wrote that soon we would meet and it would be as he was never away. He said I would learn of him by just closing my eyes and thinking. He went on "You'll feel me kiss you and hold you just as I feel you close to me tonight." He expressed that he, my mother and brother, Larry, visit each other in their hearts almost every hour that he has been away and that it's not hard when you love each other the way we do. He explained to me that we will be together again to "stay in a world where little people like you shall never know hate, fear or desperation; A world upon which the spirit of our lord, Jesus Christ walks unchallenged by foolish men." He ends by saying, "Welcome my darling daughter and may God bless you and keep you safe until my return."

Well, the war finally ended and my mother looked in he newspaper everyday for what ships were returning from Europe, hoping upon hope dad would be on one of them. Little did she know that back in England, dad was walking across an airstrip and an officer called out to him, "Hey Doc, wanna go home?" In a heartbeat dad was escorted to a plane filling up with men on their way home. He didn't even have a chance to let mom know. When he finally landed in New York, he called her. She had no idea where he was and when the phone rang casually picked it up. It was dad and he said, "Mary, I'm in New York but tomorrow I'll be in Chicago. Will you pick me up?".... The world grew bright again, the love story would continue.

My sister Cathy was born in 1949. Dad opened up his practice in Obstetrics and Gynecology in Berwyn, Illinois. He became a

Diplomat of The American College of Obstetrics and Gynecology, a Founding Fellow of the American Committee on Maternal Welfare, a Fellow of the American College of Surgeons, and a Fellow of the International College of Surgeons. He was on the Board of Directors of MacNeal Memorial Hospital in Berwyn, Illinois and a lecturer for the University of Illinois. He and

Figure 53. Dr. Lawrence and Mary Sykora, Silver Wedding Anniversary.

mother enjoyed traveling, all sports, and especially a lifetime of golf together. The two of them were a force of nature and an inspiration to all of us that loved them. Theirs was a true and deep love affair that lasted 70 years. Every time my father spoke of the war it was never about the horror of it but rather about the brave soldiers who fought it. He never again liked mountains, would only buy American built cars and turned way from war movies.

My wonderful, gentle, quick witted father passed away in my mother's arms surrounded by his three children in the early morning hours of March 6, 2009. He was the first man I ever loved and the man I loved the longest.

SPIES AND DARKENED WINDOWS
Pattie Jo (PJ) Tower

Long Island, New York was far from the "War Fronts," yet it did play a part in the happenings of World War II. Many recall the event when German U-boats landed agents on the shores of Long Island. The United States Coast Guard was kept busy on the land and sea of the Long Island South Shore area.

One incident involved my family. We had moved up from St. Augustine, Florida and lived in a "house of three." This meant there were three houses grouped together sort of like a spot on the end of a stick. We had a slip in our backyard to dock a boat in peace time and the slip went for about a hundred yards or so, ending out into Long Island's Great South Bay. Across the water were Oak and Fire Islands and then the Atlantic Ocean.

While in Florida, we became used to hearing "whump, whump, whump" at night and knew either depth charges or bombs were being dropped on or near German submarines that were close to the coast. In those days, subs needed to surface in order to recharge their batteries and get fresh air, or so we were told. Some nights we heard the distant "whumps" while living in our new home location in New York!

In wartime, it was required that all windows must have blackout curtains so that no light would show through in the night. One night our phone rang and it was the air raid warden complaining to my mother that he could see a spot of light escaping from our front window. Thus, we must have torn the blackout curtain or were careless. All the party-line people shared this conversation and many joined in to tell mother how to fix the situation. Although grateful for the advice, mother was annoyed and demanded the warden visit her. The next day he did. He gave mother a warning citation for a blackout curtain violation.

With no one listening in, mother mentioned: we do not get any gas ration stamps and our neighbor goes out after midnight in his Chris Craft about two times per week? Where does he get the gas? Why do we get a citation on our one mistake on the blackout curtain, one complaint, and yet this neighbor can burn a bright fire in an old oil drum two times a week? What is so special about our neighbors?

The warden told my mother – it is being taken care of and for her to mind her own business!

You don't say that to my mother. She was steamed!

While our neighbors were always friendly when we met either in town, in their store, working in the yard or bicycling, we really didn't see that much of each other. But, if one were ill – we would all help each other. We just felt good that way.

One day I had stopped by the neighbors' store on my way home from school. I did this often to help carry their groceries home. The Mrs. was upset and asked me to stop by her house, go in and tell her husband to hang up the phone and get himself down to the store. He was late and she needed to get home and "fix the meal." "Go in and get him," she asked.

When I got to their house – no one answered the front door and no one answered the back door. So, I went in the unlocked back door looking for the husband. I heard a radio being played but the words were in German. I saw the telephone, unplugged from the wall. And then I saw the husband cleaning parts of a "stripped-down" machine gun. It looked like the "tommy guns" seen in the movies. I yelled and he looked up and yelled something back and started moving towards me very fast. I yelled, "Your wife is mad at you," as I ran out of the house, across our yards and into my house. I grabbed my mother – who now was scared because I was scared and the man came into our kitchen. Mother picked up a cutlery knife and waved it. He yelled at me. Then it became very quiet.

"I could not hear what you said," he said to me. I repeated his wife's message. He said "Thank you." And, then he left, muttering in German.

Mother then said, "That's it? Tell me everything." Afterwards she called a friend to come over and they talked in private; not on the party line phone.

I won't bore you with the details of the following events other than to say: Mother went to into New York City and visited the

Federal Bureau of Investigation (FBI). Mother was clear about the neighbors' night adventures and the kitchen scene. She was told to relax and was ushered out of the building with no other reassuring comments.

Results? The same day mother visited the FBI, we were changed from a party line to a private phone line! This made it easier for the FBI to listen in on our phone conversations. The neighbor became very friendly, bringing us an apple pie and such now and then.

After the Victory in Europe Day (V-E Day) celebration began in the United States, our neighbors visited us and told us they were German Jews. The German government had held their son hostage and sent the parents here; set them up in business by providing funds for a store, a home, boat, etc. When these people arrived in the United States, they went first to the FBI and turned themselves in. The FBI used them as DOUBLE AGENTS! Yes, their son survived the war and he was finally reunited with his parents.

So while we, the Tower family, were safe in the United States of America, safe because so many others gave up their lives and limbs and mental health for our safety – some of us had minor incidents back here at home. My experience is minor but it gives special meaning to the saying: Freedom Isn't Free.

Figure 54. American troops of the 27th and 31st Infantry Regiments parading through Vladivostok. World War I Signal Corps Photograph, in the public domain.

DAD, RUSSIA, AND THE WORLD WAR

Josie Vine
Traverse City, Michigan

My dad was 80 years old when he wrote his memoirs of WWI, and I am amazed he could remember so much after all these years.

It was 1918. The war was almost over but President Woodrow Wilson was persuaded by Great Britain and France to intervene in the civil war in Russia. He sent 5,000 American troops to war at the North Russian Port of Archangel on the White Sea. Then he sent another 8,000 troops to fight in Vladivostok on the Bay of the Golden Horn in Eastern Siberia. Long after their buddies in France had gone home, these doughboys continued to fight a desperate, bloody, forgotten war.

These American soldiers were called "The Polar Bears", named that because it was said nothing but a polar bear could live in 60° below zero weather. They lived in box cars and built blockhouses out of logs which I suppose housed supplies and machine guns.

My dad never talked about WWI or what they did day after day. So, when this memoir writing happened, we had some idea of what it was like for them. Political reasons were never discussed. There were many reasons why these soldiers came to Russia, but, only one reason they stayed – to intervene in a civil war to see who would govern the New Russia – the largest country in the world. The militant wing of the Provisional Social Democratic Labor Party (Communists), who called themselves Bolsheviks, wanted to reorganize Russia. They were wicked and ruthless and perceived as weak. However, weak they were not!!

Winston Churchill's comment to the House of Commons on May 11, 1953 was an interesting observation, "The day will come when it will be recognized without a doubt throughout the civilized world that the strangling of Bolshevism at birth would have been an untold blessing to the human race."

As time wore on and fighting ended, the Yanks were scattered in many different towns along the Ussuri River in October, as the fierce Siberian winter awaited them. Virtually all of Siberia is north of the United States and half of it above the 60th parallel. It is an Arctic cold, deadly and merciless. The windless air increased the danger of frostbite. A soldier could spit and see it ping from the frozen surface. A young American lieutenant stationed at a remote village saw wolves approaching his command post. Before he fired his .45 into the starry night he realized the wolves were gray coated Russian soldiers crawling through the blizzard, because their feet were frozen.

So, I am leaving you with a little bit of history and a glimpse of what their lives were like. Following is the memoir of Robert A. Burns; the man who was my father and raised me during the WWII years. I hope you enjoy his WWI Story.

MEMORIES AND INCIDENTS OF MY SERVICE IN THE U.S. ARMY PFC ROBERT A. BURNS, CO. B 310TH ENGINEERS 85TH DIVISION HARRISON, MICHIGAN

I was ordered to report on my birthday, April 27, 1918, to the depot in Harrison, Michigan. Twelve other men were at the depot when I arrived. A mistake had been made in the date, so we were sent home and told to return on April 29th at the same time.

We enjoyed an uneventful train ride to Battle Creek. We marched from the train to the barracks, where we were inducted and issued uniforms.

We were replacement troops and put in with men who had been in training all winter and were about ready to go "across the pond." I was in Camp Custer during my training for the Army. My training consisted mostly of Kitchen Police (KP), a job you generally get for making mistakes in training! One of my early mistakes was made in practice throwing of hand grenades. I did not hear the instructions from the Sergeant and thought I was supposed to throw the grenade as far as possible. Instead, you were to hit an imaginary trench. So, I got KP duty. In fact, I was on KP duty six weeks of the three months I was training before going across the pond.

I did not get any military training, except for training on the rifle range where I got a perfect score on rapid-fire.

In July we were shipped out of Camp Custer to New York Harbor. There we boarded an old British freighter and went across the Big Pond, as we called the Atlantic. We landed in Liverpool, England, fourteen days later, about the worst fourteen days of my life! I was sea-sick all of the transit. I was still on K.P. The English food was poor. The potatoes were boiled with the skins on and sickened me more than ever as they did not look clean, nor smell good.

We were marched from the ship on slippery cobblestone pavement in the dark to the railroad station and lined up on the loading platform. We must have stood there for hours as it finally began to get daylight. We were then taken to Camp Aldershot (nicknamed Cowshot by us), a military rest camp, all tents, eight men to a tent, with bedrolls and not room for one more man. We were in Camp Cowshot for about three weeks, resting and getting inspected about three or four times a week. One day we had to line up and sit down on the ground, take off one shoe and sock, put the sock on one hand and sit there until the English General came to look us over. After about two hours, a big old gentleman came walking along looking everywhere but at us. That was the inspection!!

I applied for a leave of absence to go visit London. I had to go alone as my buddies had already gone to London. I found Pick-A-Dilly Square and took in a few sights, but had to return to camp before seeing very much. In a few days, we were boarded on a train and took off across England and Scotland to Glasgow. It was at night and the train was not allowed to have any lights and no smoking as England was being bombed in August 1918.

We were marched from the railroad to another British freighter for our trip to North Russia, but none of us knew where we were going. This ship was not as bad as the first one, so I did not get seasick. In a few days we pulled into a harbor on Iceland and took on some supplies. I saw them board one big fish about the size of a man, a sea bass I was told. I thought we might have a fish supper, but that was my last view of the fish!

This harbor was a beautiful sight from the ship; a group of buildings all painted white along the water, and from there, the land sloped upward as far as we could see, covered with green grass and not a tree of any kind in sight.

I must have improved in my training, as I don't recall being on kitchen police on this trip. Our destination was not told to us, and we did not find out where we were going until we got there. We finally came to the mouth of a large river, the Dvina, which was one mile wide. We started up the channel which seemed like several miles, when we began to see buildings which looked like a city. We found out it was Archangel, Russia, the most northern port in Russia.

We unloaded on a dock that was like a bridge built on piling. They marched us off across the river to an old Army camp with lots of barracks.

Some infantry companies were marched farther on to the railroad and were loaded onto boxcars. The boxcars were small about half the size of ours. These boxcars pulled out of town toward the front, and through some error, were then taken too far and were riddled with machine gun fire. There was a heavy casualty list and many deaths. We were never able to find out how many, or the cause of the accident.

We soon found out that this was an old Russian Army depot at Archangel. It consisted of frame constructed warehouses about 80 feet by 250 feet, with hip roof and about 10 foot high walls. These buildings were spaced 50 feet or more apart and covered an area of one mile square, which was enclosed by a board fence ten feet high. This fence was solid all smooth on the outside. There were large solid wooden gates in this wall at intervals. Our job for the first month or two was to repair these warehouses, fences and gates. Also, we put ceilings in some of them and insulated them with hemp or sisal or some material that came in large bales. These weighed 250 lbs. and were hard to handle.

Some of our engineers discovered that this warehouse that we had insulated contained the British Army rum and whiskey they issued to their soldiers every day at the evening meal, and they included the American troops in the rum issue. I was a teetotaler and never took a drink of liquor all during my service, so would not go through the line to get my issue of rum. My friend Jack Noricki, urged me to give my rum to him. Jack would not take any chances on getting it so he always said "Mine and Burns's", when he came through the lineup.

During all this time, the days were getting shorter and the nights longer, and it was getting colder all the time. We were issued some heavy wool undershirts and wool socks; also a sheepskin lined overcoat which came down to my ankles and was very heavy but warm. I was able to send mine home and also put one of the curved-handled Russian axes in the package with the coat.

At one time, I had 80 Russian women under my charge to clean an area in front of a machine gun blockhouse we had built in the edge of a forest. Their trees were like our spruce and balsam and looked like they had been planted. They were about ten feet high and the trunks were all from four to six inches in diameter. We were several days getting them cut down and hauled away by hand.

These Russian women were good people and while there were no beauties among them they could do a lot of work. The Army hired them as we were short handed. I had another detail at the hospital where the women did the work digging holes for toilet waste from the hospital. I had no interpreter, so it was hard to make them know what was to be done. Surprisingly the ground was not frozen very deep, and we soon got a hole ten feet deep dug. The soil was sandy with stair steps up one side so they could walk up with the dirt in pails. It was piled up and enough used to cover the waste each day. The women had felt boots without any rubbers. They wore several layers of quilted robes or dresses that came down to their knees.

This blockhouse we cleared in front of finally was finished and a machine gun installed in it. My friend Jack and I were picked to guard it so the enemy could not come in and occupy it before the infantry could get there. Neither one of us knew how to operate a machine gun so we decided to learn before the enemy might show up. We finally found out how to operate it and shot a few bursts. I expected we would be punished but nothing happened. We did not want to be out there alone after dark and were getting ready to try the gun again when the infantry showed up with the men assigned to that blockhouse.

While we were billeted at Backaritza, we fixed up an old barracks and made a basketball court in it. It had a few holes in the wooden floor which we filled with dirt and had lots of fun and several different teams. This was getting late in the fall. I made the Company B team and we played Company C to determine the champions. They had a center that was seven feet tall. I could stand up straight under his out stretched arm. He was their center and I was center for our team. I could never reach the ball on the tip off so I would try to guess where he was going to knock the ball and beat their men to it. It did not work very well, but we did win the game.

We had been in the barracks at Bakaritza just out of Archangel all this time and got the word about November 15th that the Armistice had been signed on November 11, 1918. As we were frozen in, no more ships could come into Archangel until spring. We knew we were in for a long wait before we could get home. They were not going to tell us the war was over but it leaked out, so we decided we would have to make the best of it as we were near the Arctic Circle. The days kept getting shorter and nights longer. The winter cold was setting in more every day with hardly ever any sunshine. While we were still in the barracks, my friend Tourville was sick and couldn't get any rest on the hard wooden bunks, so I decided to go out in search of some hay or straw to soften up his bed. The roads were made of wood on piling about 4 or 5 feet above the ground. I never did find out whether it was marshy ground or roads just built up high to get them by in deep snow, which got to be four feet deep on the level.

I walked about a mile out this road and came to a cluster of buildings where Russian people were living. But I had a hard time trying to tell them what I wanted. Finally, one gentleman took me into his house and barn and I showed him what I wanted. Their buildings were house and barn together, built of logs. The first floor was about six feet up and the livestock was on this floor. The second floor was like a hayloft and this is where I found my hay. It looked like what we call marsh-hay. I tried to pay him for it but he wouldn't take any of my rubles. I had a little American money in silver, about $1.00. I think he seemed glad to take that. He helped me tie up a big bundle of hay with my rope and I put it on my back and got back to the barracks.

Speaking of rubles and money, I might as well mention right now that most of us would not take our pay, as the Army wanted to pay us off with rubles at the rate of 50 rubles to one $5.00 bill of American money. We found out that we could get 100 rubles for a $5.00 bill in American money in Archangel. I did not accept any of my $30.00 per month pay until I was discharged. After paying insurance and allotment to my mother and a few other deductions they took out of us, I only had $7.00 net pay per month coming to me. As our expedition was under British command, and we were issued cigarettes like their soldiers were. I did not smoke cigarettes but happened to be wise enough to take my issue which was two packages a week. They were a British brand and not liked by our troops but they smoked them. In fact, I had no trouble selling mine. We played cards using cigarettes to bet with in place of money, as all we had was paper money (rubles). At one time I had 320 packs of cigarettes coming to me on paper. I forgot what the card game was called but it was fun. This buddy got in debt to me 160 packs and wanted to play me a game double or nothing so I did, and won. He was all the rest of the winter trying to get even. I would loan him some packs to play with.

The days continued to get shorter until we had about three hours of daylight. While we could work at some things in the dark, we began to have a lot of time to kill in the dark.

We were told that we were on our Front Line of defense and that we were north of Archangel and the Front was a line running east from Divina River. We had fortified with block houses and trenches, a small village near the river on the railroad front. Our village was called Tulgas. We billeted in boxcars near the depot on a railroad siding. A stone building with a few windows was the depot. It had a big thermometer on it, and I would always look at it every time I went past it. As near as I could tell it was 40 degrees below zero.

I remember an incident while we were digging trenches at Tulgas on the front; we ran into potato pits and found a few potatoes about the size of walnuts in each pit. One pit had about a peck of these small potatoes and they sure were good. We had not had any fresh vegetables for six months or more. These pits were about six or eight feet deep, four foot square at the bottom. They were built of wood and slanted up to a top of two and one half foot square feet, with a heavy wood lid on them. The trench we were digging ran right into one of these pits and by looking around we found several other pits. I am afraid the potato crop was very short in 1919 in North Russia as I suppose these were seed potatoes we found.

One morning we were routed out of bed at 6:00 a.m. and had to answer roll call outside. The officers had decided to find out who had stolen whiskey from the warehouses and were going to punish the whole company by a report every morning until someone told who did it. I told the sergeant I did not drink, I did not steal any whiskey, and refused to be punished for something I did not do. I would not report for anymore roll calls at 6:00 am. He said I better report to the captain before I got in trouble so I went to the captain's boxcar right away.

I found him asleep in bed with a bottle of Scotch whiskey about half full on a desk beside his bed. I told him the same thing I had told the sergeant and turned around and walked out. He did not say anything. I remained in bed the next morning when the rest of the boys rolled out for 6:00 am roll call in pitch dark, 40 degrees below zero weather. A fewer amount would report every morning until all that reported was the sergeant and corporals who would go out and say all present and accounted for and that punishment was soon cancelled.

At one of these villages we fortified, we were billeted in log buildings. These buildings were the barn, house, chicken coop, hog house and living quarters. Some of these were quite large, 40 X 60 feet I would guess. The first 6 feet from the ground up was for livestock, except one corner which contained a heating plant. This was a mammoth stone or adobe stove. The opening in it was about four feet wide, two feet high and four to six feet deep. When they built the fire of wood, they would heat the mammoth unit with a slow wood fire for several hours. The top was also stone or adobe. This whole thing would get hot and stay hot for days. They cooked and baked in it and it looked like their chickens lived on the top through the winter. We were not billeted in these buildings until the winter had passed as some Russian people were occupying them at the time.

I went past a small house one day with a big glass window on one side. Inside, an old lady sat on a chair, rocking a cradle with a baby in it, with one foot. Her other foot was operating a spinning wheel as needed. She was using both hands to take something off of the spinning wheel I believe. This is as close as I will ever come to seeing perpetual motion! I could hardly take myself away and finally got the old lady to smile at me.

While at one of these small villages which we had fortified, we were alerted that we might be attacked at any time. There were supposed to be 1,600 Bolsheviks coming toward us. I was working in a trench at the time and had set my rifle up against a post outside the trench. When the first attack came, we could hear the bullets whistling over our heads, and I was scared. I asked one of my buddies, who was not in the trench yet, to hand me my rifle. Just then an officer showed up from someplace and said, "Burns". That settled me down a little so I got out of the trench and got my gun. It made me feel a lot better, but I was not very sure that it would shoot as we had not had any practice with it.

At the end of this trench, toward where the bullets were coming from was a small shed like a hog house or chicken coop. I got up behind this and could see a man crawling toward it. I took careful aim but held my fire. We were informed to hold our fire as our own troops were coming back to the trenches. I was sure glad I had not pulled the trigger! I doubt if they shot 500 rounds at us and eventually they withdrew.

These Bolsheviks had six-inch artillery and the largest we had were three-inch guns. They would stand back out of our range and pound our fortifications to pieces, so we would have to fall back to another line of fortification.

We had learned in the winter that they had a six-inch gun mounted on a railroad car and we tried to stop that. I was on the detail of twelve engineers picked to go out around their front line to where this gun was located and blow up the railroad track so they could not use it.

We loaded up three toboggan sleds with crowbars, a tent, a stove, saws, etc. It was supposed to take us three days. They sent two Frenchmen on skis ahead of us, through the thick woods to make a trail for our toboggans. We also had gun cotton to carry in knapsacks on our backs. I think I had twelve pieces about half the size of a cigar box. I was not instructed how to use this but was told how to fasten it on the railroad rails. Another buddy was to set the gun cotton off.

The first day out on this trip was slow and hard work as the track through the woods was tough. The first night out, we pitched our tent and set up an airtight heater or stove and rolled into bed on top of about four feet of snow. We had built a fire in the stove and although it was way below zero we didn't mind the cold. We were tired and hot from exhaustion.

The next day was similar to the first day but we made fair progress. The night was a repeat of the first, but we were getting toughened to the work. The third day we were supposed to reach our destination (the six-inch gun) about noon. That day a runner on skis caught up with us with orders to return to camp, no reasons given. So, we lightened up our heavy loads on the toboggans and took off for home.

I roamed around this village and discovered there had been a good sized sawmill there. I also got to see a hand-powered sawmill in operation. The tree to be sawed into lumber was trimmed and the top cut off at about the six inch diameter of the tree, now log. This log was hoisted up on two horses or wooden posts. The log was then squared by broad axes. The saw which was identical to our ice saws, was started one man on top with the help of a man on the ground to pull the saw up and then force it down through the log. I saw some of the boards they had cut, which were about an inch thick and full width of the log, also full length. They were not working, so I don't know how long it would take to saw off one board. I saw one building with these rough sawed boards on it. They did not square the boards on the sides but used them full width on the log. Some would be twelve inches wide on one end and six inches on the other end.

We were building a block house in one of the villages on the front line. The logs were all peeled about six or eight inches in diameter at the top and ten to twelve inches at the butt. I was notching and grooving logs at the building site when the sergeant came after me to help carry one of the logs up to the building. There were five or six men standing around the log they wanted moved. This made me disgusted so I walked up to the end of the log, the small end, picked it up and said, "What are you waiting for?" I started to walk off with it before they could take hold of it. I had quite a reputation as a axe man on those log machine gun nests. It was all rough work.

In the middle of the winter while in the railroad front, I became lousy. They were about the size of a kernel of wheat and quite plentiful! They had bath houses made of logs. The inside was built up two feet high on one side of the room and filled with stones. A fire was build under the stones and they were heated very hot. The fire was then pulled out and you took your own water in pails and threw on the stones which made a lot of steam. After steaming myself good, I bathed myself and dried off. All this time I had been boiling my underwear. I took a whole day off to do this but I got rid of the lice and was not bothered again.

While we were away from Archangel, during the winter, someone had built a log foundation on top of the ice on the river and laid a railroad track on top of this to run the railroad trains across the river. There was no bridge.

The spring came gradually, the days became longer, and the first we knew there were no more nights, all daylight. North of us a few 100 miles, the sun shone at midnight. When we boarded the ship to come home, it was the last of May. It was daylight all night long. One of the most awe inspiring sights for me was when the ice started going out of the big Divina River. The four foot or more of snow that had been on the ground all winter had melted and all the small streams were overflowing their banks. This made flood conditions near the streams and raised the river so the ice broke loose from the banks.

I stood looking across the river and saw a man with a horse and sleigh out about a quarter of a mile or so on the ice. All at once the man started whipping the horse and shouting. I couldn't tell why, but finally I could see the ice moving very slowly down stream. That whole body of ice, four feet thick before the thaw, had started to move. I could see the man, horse and sleigh still running as hard as they could toward the other shore. The river was supposed to be a mile wide, but must not have been at this place, because I watched them get off on the other shore.

A large handmade barge (wooden) had been tied up on my side of the river all winter. I would guess it to be 20 feet wide by 60 feet long. The ends were made of large timbers sloping from the water up to the top of the sides. I did not see how they would dare leave a good looking barge in a dangerous place like that. I was back to this place two or three days later and all that was left of the barge was slivers! It had been crushed into toothpick size pieces.

We were detailed to repair a bridge on a dirt road near the river about one quarter mile away. The road was flooded right up close to the bridge. On each side they had moved in some large timbers close to the bridge but not used them. The powers that be decided that if we could get a horse out to the bridge it could be used to move the large timbers p to the bridge and fix it. I was detailed to row the boat with one other man. The boat was like a lifeboat, about eighteen feet long, and five feet deep in the center, with curved sides and no seats. We had a hard time getting the horse to step into the boat. The man handling the horse could sure make him understand what he wanted him to do. It was very difficult to keep the horse from rocking the boat but the fellow handling the horse was an expert. I can't remember the man's name, but I believe he was a blacksmith and shod horses. The other rower and I finally got our load out to the bridge and took the empty boat back. They said the water would go down quick and they could probably walk out on the road in a few days.

While we were waiting at the barracks at Backaritza near Archangel, for our ships to come to take us home, some of the boys went swimming in the river. This was the latter part of May. I did not try it.

But the previous fall, while we were billeted in the barracks at Backariza, we were allowed passes to go to Archangel. During the long evenings there was not much to see or do. But, we discovered there was a skating rink. When I was a kid in Greenview, Illinois, I loved to skate on Grove Creek, a small creek that ran through the edge of town.

We met some young Russian girls at the skating rink and enjoyed several evenings skating with them. We had to talk to them by sign language. I was able to get along pretty good with the young lady about twenty years old and used to walk home with her after the rink closed. We had to walk through part of the business district of Archangel. She never invited me into her home. We had to report in a 1:00 am at the barracks so I would sometimes have to run part of the way home to get there on time.

I tried to find this girl in May when we came back to these same barracks, to wait for our ship to come and take us home. I never could find her, but when our ship got there and they loaded us on I went up on deck. There were quite a few Russian people on the dock to bid us goodbye, and low and behold, my girl was there. She had a picture or something in a big envelope and waved it at me. I tried hard to get off the boat to get the envelope but they would not let me off. I went back on deck and had to be satisfied with waving goodbye to her, as we pulled out right away for home. I never did find out this girl's name.

We were accused of mutiny in North Russia, we did a bit of kicking and complaining for having to continue in combat about eight months after the Armistice was signed.

We did not have to worry about being attacked by submarines on our trip coming home and it was an uneventful voyage to Le Havre, France. We were unloaded there and marched two miles or more to a rest camp.

It had just rained a heavy shower and the mud was up to our ankles. After a few days rest we were loaded on a good American ship and brought home. I believe it took us six days to come home. It was a good voyage. I had no more seasickness and was not on kitchen police even once. We were unloaded at New York and shipped right out to Columbus, Ohio where we were discharged.

By not taking my pay while in Russia, I was paid over $300 as severance pay. With this I paid for a Ford Model T touring car, a month or two after reaching home on the farm, nine miles north of Harrison, Michigan.

Counting that winter 1918 and 1919, I played basketball for 28 years. Not full seasons every year but I played on undefeated teams. One year in Greenview, Illinois, and several years at Harrison, Michigan.

I would like to share one other item of interest. While in Russia, I noticed around the railroad yards stacks of what looked to be very large gates. Finally, I inquired what they were used for. They told me they hooked them up together forming a portable fence which was used to stop the snow drifts. After returning to America and home in Harrison I recalled what a help these gates were in Russia, and could be in this part of the country. So, I mentioned it to a man on the County Road Commission, Sam Bruce, that if we could use something like a picket fence only one that would roll up it would stop some of the large drifted areas we have up here. He said he would give it some thought. Well, the very next year, what to my surprise did I start seeing along certain areas but picket fences which could be rolled up, or what we now call snow fences. So, maybe in this one case we did get something from Russia that they discovered first!

Many other incidents occurred which I cannot recall but I will add to these if I remember them. I did not think of writing these until I had passed my 80th birthday.

MILITARY POLICE IN A SECRET CITY

Ambrose A. Weber
US Army, Kingsley, Michigan

I was born in Kingsley, Michigan, one of eleven children. Now at 92 years of age, I am pleased to report that nine of those eleven are still living. Four of my siblings served in the military during World War II; myself in the Army as a Military Police, Clarence in the Infantry in Germany, Ray also in the Infantry in Germany, and Jay in the Army as an electrical technician serving in the Pacific.

After the attack on Pearl Harbor, I was drafted. On December 31, 1941, I arrived in Battle Creek, Michigan at which time I received my uniform; although, it was three sizes too large for me. My service began on January 2, 1942. I started Military Police (MP) training the next day, training in Fort Custer, Michigan. After three months I shipped out to South Carolina, although my actual orders came out of Georgia. I ended up in Casual Company, and served on various MP security duties all along the East Coast of the United States. This duty was a quiet deal for me as there were no significant incidents during any of my watches.

After my duties along the coastline, I was sent to Oakridge, Tennessee where we guarded the outer perimeters of an area controlled by the Manhattan District, US Army Corps of Engineers. This facility at Oakridge, Tennessee, was known as the "secret city build overnight." Most of the people working there did not know about the "bomb," each

Figure 55. Security reminder on Billboard at the Manhattan Project's Oak Ridge, Tennessee facility during WWII. US Government Photo.

only knew their specific duty and were not aware of the entire operation. This facility was so secret that Vice President Truman did

159

not even know of its existence until he was inaugurated. After President Roosevelt's death, he was briefed on the Manhattan Project and the experiments associated with the development of the atomic bombs. He was then the one that had to make the final decisions regarding the use of nuclear bombs as weapons of war; a decision that quickly lead to the Japanese surrender and ultimately the end of World War II. I was on MP duty at one of the several entrances to the Oakridge facility when the Japs surrendered. It was only many years later that we learned of the role that Oakridge served within the "Manhattan Project" and the true uranium enrichment capabilities developed in the facilities we were charged with securing. Just a few days after the Japanese surrender in 1945, I was discharged from military duty. My military service for my country lasted 38 months.

I returned to work at General Motors in Pontiac, Michigan and worked there for the next 33 ½ years. I married Ruth Snowden and we shared 63 years together. Ruth and I have two children, Gary and Helen.

I am very close with my brother Clarence and he calls me every day. I am proud that his military story has been featured in newspaper articles. As mentioned, Clarence served as an infantryman in Europe. He was in the winter-time Battle of the Bulge in France. He participated in the landing at Omaha Beach and the invasion of Normandy. He talks of the men involved, the quiet nerves on the packed ship as it approached the invasion and the loss of men as they scaled the ships and entered the water. All were bloodied either with the raining fire of the German gunners or experiencing the loss of life of many comrades. Everyone was scared, as any human would be. Death and devastation was all around the beachhead as thousands of troops were killed, many needed to be stepped over and some functioned as shields for the living; all were respected and honored by their fellow soldiers. My brother was wounded, being shot in the leg during subsequent battle in France.

Time heals the wounds of war, although my brother had experienced nightmares after he returned, one time actually jumping through a window while having a dream about his terrifying war experiences. He looks back at his experience with amazement for our forces perseverance through incredibly challenging actions, protecting life and liberty.

My experience and those of my brothers were all very different during WWII. We all went to war for all the right reasons, to protect the freedoms we all enjoyed and to protect our nation. Together, all of the Allied Forces, each and every individual, with their sacrifices and bravery, accomplished an amazing feat; securing freedom and winning World War II.

Figure 56. Workers at the Oak Ridge Facility in Oakridge Tennessee celebrate the Japanese surrender and the end of World War II. US Government Photo.

Editor's Note: Related Stories

John Edmond Kelly

In the following pages, we have included several additional stories from contributors beyond our Bay Ridge Community. These include a story from the 101st Airborne from John Peterson, now residing in a Michigan Veterans home in Grand Rapids, an as well as several additional stories discussing how our war years have affected subsequent generations.

The first of these stories is from my granddaughter Sterling who married an active duty US Navy Seabee and Civil Engineer Corp (CEC) Officer, Lieutenant Gregory C. Kirk in early 2007. Sterling soon became active with the Washington, DC, area CEC Officer's Spouse Club where she met the Navy's senior CEC Officer Admiral Gregory Shear at a function held at his home, hosted by his wife Marlene Shear. She talked to him about her WWII veteran grandfather, meeting Greg, and all about the 31st Seabee Reunions. As a result, ADM Shear and his wife asked her to submit an article telling her story for their Honey Buzz Newsletter, published in November of 2007. The story that follows is the result of that request.

Her writing shows me that she understands much of what I know we all understand…we value each other, we value our service to our country, we value today's active military, we value our families… and we always will.

With great pride, I share this article and hope you all understand that due to the sacrifices of many brave Americans, Sterling is blessed as the wife of a CEC Seabee, the niece of a retired Navy Reserve Commander, the granddaughter of both myself, a WWII Veteran Seabee, and Solomon Meyer an Army Medic that served on the USS *Hope* (AH-7).

I share a thought from Sterling's heartfelt writings… I hope you again see "the glimmer of an earlier youth appear in old friends eyes"…

With Great Respect…John E. Kelly

Figure 57. John E. Kelly with his Granddaughter Sterling, Lieutenant Gregory Kirk, USN, and Commander Thomas J. Kelly, USNR. US Naval Academy. Photo by Janice Kelly Meyer.

ONCE A SEABEE, ALWAYS A SEABEE

Sterling Janice Kirk
US Navy Spouse, Traverse City, Michigan

Many of you own the Seabee history book *Can Do!* On the back cover there is a photograph of two men chopping coral with sledge hammers. The left handed man wearing glasses is John E. Kelly and I am proud to say that he is my grandfather. Like many men in WWII he was eager to join the war effort and serve his country. He was an underage left handed man with terrible eyesight, which at that time could make you ineligible for active duty military service. However, the man testing the vision screenings believed my grandfather was faking his poor vision because his testing went so badly. They let him serve his country by chopping coral on the island of Tinian with the 38th Seabees to prepare the runway for the atomic bombs. At the end of the war they transferred my grandfather to the 31st Seabees where they served in Iwo Jima and at the destroyed city of Nagasaki handling reconstruction efforts and cleaning up nuclear waste at the bomb's hypocenter.

As a very young girl I can recall gazing at a menacing statue on my grandfather's shelf and being a bit frightened and confused. It looked a little like a bumble bee but I couldn't figure out why it was gripping construction tools and was armed with a gun. When I reached up to touch it, it wobbled back and forth and I thought for sure it was going to come to life and sting me! I asked my grandmother what that scary bee was and she said, "Oh that's not scary. You're Grandpa used to be one of those when he was in the Navy." This answer did not explain any of the questions that I already had. Instead it also left me wondering how in the world my grandfather used to be a bee and was now a human today?

As the years passed I learned about my grandfather's service in the Navy where he was a member of the 31st and 38th Seabee units during WWII. When I was in my early teenage years my Grandfather used his "Can Do!" spirit and decided to find the members of his old battalions in an effort to organize their first reunion since they were discharged. I did not understand what a battalion was or what these men had done. What I did understand was that this was extremely important to my grandfather and even though it was a long and difficult process he did not give up!

In 1994 my family hosted the first reunion in Washington, DC. As the guests arrived it was amazing to see the swell of emotions that flowed through the room. There were veterans that hadn't seen each other in 50 years, widows that came just to meet the people that their late husbands used to speak so highly of, children and grandchildren that came along with their relatives and others that came alone to pay tribute to a lost loved one in their life. The stories that I heard were incredible but what sticks in my mind most today was seeing the glimmer of an earlier youth appear in old friends' eyes as they were reunited. It truly was amazing! The first reunion was a hit and they decided right then and there that they would try to make this an annual event for as long as they all had left to live.

I attended many of these reunions but the reunion that changed my life the most was in October 2005. At the last minute I decided not to go because I just had too many things going on in Michigan involving my business and work schedule. My family went without me and had a wonderful time hosting the reunion. It was at the Friday night social that Lieutenant Greg Kirk came to give a speech on what the Seabees were doing today in the world. Throughout the course of the evening Greg met my grandfather and mother and wouldn't you know it, my mom said "Hey, could you have somebody email my daughter and tell her what a fun time she missed?" He of course said he would do that, although he was feeling a bit reluctant about what he had just committed too. True to Navy form, he followed through with her request.

A few days later I received an email from Greg. I didn't know anything about him except that he was a Seabee and that my mother and grandfather apparently approved of him since they had set us up. We both must have been a bit unsure of what to say to each other because I think our first five emails were about drywall and painting. Apparently these were very comfortable topics for a Seabee. Naturally our conversation topics changed and we decided to meet each other in December of 2005. Our first meeting was wonderful and I instantly had a hunch that I had met the man that I was supposed to spend the rest of my life with..... Nine months later Greg asked me to be his wife and I gladly accepted. We were married at the United States Naval Academy Chapel on April 14, 2007.

Now that I am a Civil Engineer Corps spouse I have a new perspective on what my grandfather did and accomplished through the reunions he organized. I can see that these men were there for each other and stood united in WWII just as they still do today.

Figure 58. Sterling and Lieutenant Gregory Kirk, just married, on the steps on the Naval Academy Chapel, Annapolis, Maryland, 14 April, 2007. Photo by Janice Kelly Meyer.

In reality our spouses are not any different. It's just that today we are much younger than the veterans of WWII are now and many of us have a very busy schedule raising families and building careers. Sometimes we find it hard to attend our monthly coffee's, lunch bunch, picnics and various events, but when we are old and our bodies demand us to slow down we will long to connect with the people that we are surrounded with today. We will want to remember the best days of our lives that we are living right now and wouldn't think twice about traveling from Arizona to Washington DC for a chance to have coffee and perhaps dinner with some old friends that once defended each other's lives and country in their youth.

My name is Sterling Kirk and I am the wife of Lieutenant Gregory C. Kirk, granddaughter of WWII Veteran Seabee John E.

Kelly and niece of Retired United States Navy Reserve Commander Thomas J. Kelly. I can't remember a time in my life when I didn't know the words to the Seabee Song or the pride a family feels by being a part of the United States Navy. My Grandfather deserves a giant THANK YOU for instilling the "CAN DO!" spirit in me when I was a young girl. My experiences have taught me that whether you're a veteran, an officer, a family member or spouse one thing will always remain the same. Once you've been a Seabee, you will always be a Seabee!

★ ★ ★ ★ ★

Figure 59. WWII Navy Recruiting Poster.

THE INSPIRATIONS OF VETERANS

Thomas J. Kelly
US Navy Reserve, Saginaw, Michigan

I was born in 1950, three or four years into the post-WWII baby boom. I grew up among a cadre of veterans, my father serving in the Navy, five uncles with Army service, a grandfather that served in the WWI Army Signal Corps and another that was a merchant mariner. I also knew I had ancestors that fought in the French and Indian War, the American Revolution, the War of 1812, and with Michigan's 1st United States Lancers during the Civil War. In spite of starting college in the milieu of the Vietnam conflict, I always assumed I would serve in the military. In October 1969, I followed in my father's footsteps and enlisted as a Quartermaster "striker" in the Naval Reserve. In the Navy, Quartermasters navigate and maneuver the ship; we have Storekeepers to perform the Army's quartermaster functions.

After a short boot camp at Great Lakes Naval Training Center, and two weeks on a destroyer escort moored to the pier in downtown Chicago, Illinois, I received active duty orders to report to Newport, Rhode Island. Studying and practicing navigation in the sunny and social Newport summer, right in the heart of the 1970 32nd America's Cup defense, with frequent sails out into Narragansett Bay to observe the 12-meter yachts heading out to sea for the daily competitions was a great way to start a navy career. In spite of all of Newport's distractions, I completed my Quartermaster training, volunteered for submarine duty, and moved to Groton, Connecticut to complete Sub School. Winter in "New London" allowed me to wear the essentially new, well tailored, dress blue wool uniform my father, John E. Kelly, had acquired in the week before he was discharged in 1946 (see page 44). I requested orders to a

Figure 60. USS John Marshall (SSBN-611) underway on the surface. US Navy Photo.

169

Polaris Missile Submarine and was ordered to the USS John Marshall (SSBN-611G) in January of 1971.

In that cold war era, ballistic missile submarines already carried the most significant portion of United States' strategic nuclear deterrent. These operating ships were underway two-thirds of the time maintaining their three prioritized missions: Remain undetected, maintain the capability to accurately fire their missiles within minutes, and receive national command authority communications. During my first of three, three-month long, "deterrent patrol," I qualified on my watch station, received my "dolphins" for qualifying on submarines, and volunteered for Navy diving school

I finished my two years of active duty and was transferred to the drilling reserves as a QM2 (SSDV). I continued to serve as a drilling reservist while I used the GI Bill to complete my BS in biochemistry and two years of graduate work in physiology and neuroscience. As a senior Quartermaster, I provided navigation and fire-control training at the Lansing reserve center, the USNR combat simulation training facilities in Battle Creek, Michigan, and on board the various Navy ships to which I was assigned.

While employed as a researcher at Michigan State University's College of Human Medicine, I was actively pursuing a direct commission as an Aviation Physiologist in the US Navy Medical Service Corps. Within eight weeks of my intended commissioning, that program was cancelled and I was informed that the only program with opening still available was commissioning as an Intelligence Officer. I applied and was commissioned as an Ensign in July 1980.

My first training period as a new Ensign was two weeks spent working with an Office of Naval Intelligence (ONI) command. The command focused on providing scientific intelligence to the US Navy to help in defining the technical capabilities of foreign navies. I enjoyed the mission, the work, and the professionals I worked with at ONI, and six months later I moved to the Washington area and became a full-time civilian intelligence analyst.

I have now worked as a civilian in the military intelligence field for almost 30 years and have had wonderful opportunities to understand and support almost every aspect of our Navy's mission and our nation's intelligence community. I continued to serve as an Intelligence Officer until the summer of 2007 when I retired from the Navy Reserve after 37 years and 8 months. My reserve experiences were separate from my civilian duties; I supported international war games, overseas activities, technical experiments, Inspector General duties, served as XO of a 45 member unit

Figure 61. CDR Thomas J. Kelly

supporting an overseas US Command involved in combat, and ran intelligence cells for four consecutive 'fleet battle experiments."

I have enjoyed my Navy experiences; I've seen the globe, been to sea on a score of ships, learned to better understand the world, seen our military in action in hundreds of ways, observed our government functioning at every level, and built a continuity with many of those veterans that went before me. I have been fascinated with the talents, heart, and character of the Seabee veterans that I have met while participating with the reunions of my father's WWII cohorts. I have great pride in the selfless contributions of all of the Greatest Generation, veterans and others.

Figure 62. CDR Kelly briefing current Seabee deployments to the 31st NCB Reunion in 2003.

The stories offered in this book provide an expanded insight into what these warriors, workers, widows, and visionaries gave to America and the world during that global struggle, as well as after. There continues to be evil in our world today; genocide, oppression, ignorance, slavery, violence, threat, and intolerance, and these ills will continue to bud where true freedom fails. America's ability to derail the global infection of these evils almost 70 years ago was in many ways a near thing –

our technologies helped, but it was the commitments and character of millions of individual Americans that held the day. I believe that achieving a true understanding of where we have been and who we can be as a society, by absorbing the leading inspirations from Adams to Eisenhower, and from the patriots in this book, is the best bulwark against future generations ever having to endure another such global trial.

Very Respectfully
Thomas J. Kelly
Commander, USNR (Ret)

Figure 63. CDR Thomas J. Kelly, USNR, and his father, Seabee John E. Kelly, attending John's 31st Naval Construction Battalion Reunion's Memorial Presentation in 2003.

FROM FOXHOLE TO EAGLE'S NEST

John G. Peterson
US Army, Newaygo, Michigan

I was born John G. Peterson, in Wichita Fall, Texas on July 26th 1919. My mother, Margret Ann Stuckey Peterson, died of tuberculosis when I was two years old and my father Carl Peterson took me to my grandmother, Bertha Kelly Stuckey in Warren Pennsylvania. My grandmother and grandfather were no longer married and my grandfather lived in St. Louis, Missouri, on Butterfly Lake. I was left by my father to be raised by my maternal grandmother. I lived with my grandmother until I graduated high school.

When growing up I would spend my summers in Middletown, Ohio with my Cousin Ruey and his family. Ruey and I were like brothers. One time my Grandfather invited Ruey and I to come to Farmington, Missouri to spend the summer. When we got there he gave us guns and put us up in a cabin on his back 40, left to fend for ourselves. We were there for six weeks and became very close.

I had never seen my father while growing up. He showed up at my high school graduation ceremony in Lancaster, Ohio. At that time he lived in Saginaw, Michigan. That was when I found out that my name was not John G. Stuckey but John G. Peterson, so I began using my legal name and moved to Saginaw, Michigan to be near my father. We were never close and moving there did not change that.

While living in Saginaw, Michigan, I went ice skating at Hoyt Park and there was a girl sledding there, named Marylou Rutter. I ran into her and knocked her over. That encounter led to our beginning to date. Our first real date was to go fishing on Lake Mitchell in Cadillac. I later asked her to marry me.

After moving to Saginaw in an attempt to be close to my father, he moved to Cadillac, Michigan. After Marylou and I were married my father remarried and he had a son Steve, my half brother. Marylou and I used to take care of Steve when he was very young, often for extended periods of time.

A short time after we were married Marylou and I moved to Cincinnati, Ohio, were I was working at Wieget Cyclone Aircraft Engine Plant. We had two daughters; Margret Ann Peterson was born pre-WWII on January 16, 1943, and Debra Louise Peterson, was born post-WWII December 21, 1951. When the war started, I enlisted in the Army. When I left for war duty, Marylou and Margaret Ann (about fifteen months old) moved to Saginaw, Michigan to live with Marylou's parents.

Figure 64. John Peterson completes his "money jump" becoming a US Army Paratrooper with the 101ˢᵗ Airborne. Photo provided by John Peterson.

I enlisted in the service and was assigned duty in the infantry. My buddy Cyril (Pete) Pedersen and I did not like the infantry because they made us walk too much. We saw a notice on the bulletin board about the paratroopers looking for volunteers so we talked it over and decided to sign up together. After we signed up we were sent to Fort Benning, Georgia, for training to become a paratrooper. During Jump School you can decide at any time to drop out and go back to the infantry. (We did not think that would be a good option so we stuck it out) Once you do your last training jump you cannot drop out, you are given your wings and you are now in the Paratroopers. We were assigned to the 101ˢᵗ Airborne, the Screaming Eagles. After Jump Training we were sent overseas to England and then to Jaunay, France. That is when all hell broke loose. The Germans made a breakthrough in December. We were all dressed up to go on leave into Jaunay, France for Christmas when we were told we were not going to get to go on leave. They loaded us onto 2-

ton trucks that were heading north in the dark. As we drove through the night we did not know where we were going or what lay ahead. As daylight came we were still driving north but we were driving past all of the infantry men as they were heading south. (I was hoping that my choice to leave the infantry was a good one). They were driving us up to the front lines. We had very little ammunition and the men heading away from the front lines were handing us all of their ammo. They gave us all of the artillery rounds and ammo they had so we could fight what was coming ahead. We were taken to Bastogne, a major rail hub. We were ordered by General Eisenhower to hold Bastogne from the Germans. So the 101st Airborne and 82nd Airborne formed a circle, a combat circle, in the woods around the area of Bastogne. From then on all hell broke loose; we were in the fight of our lives.

The Germans hit us with the Panther Division of Tiger Tanks. They surrounded us in the woods in Bastogne. They could not get to us because we were in the woods and their tanks could not drive into the woods. They did however shoot off all the tops of the trees with the attempts of trying to kill us. After a while the shooting from the tanks stopped. It was very silent and we all knew what was about to happen. Through the fog we could see all the German soldiers coming around the tanks and towards us into the woods. We were in our fox holes both Easy Company and Fox Company; we set up crossfire to fight the German soldiers. They retreated; only to return again. From this point on it was just a matter of sitting in the woods holding our position, fighting off the Germans each time they came and following out orders from General Eisenhower to hold the area. That is what we were ordered to do so that is what we did. There were men being wounded and dying all around us. We sat in the mud, the blood, and the snow, and continued to fight for our country and our lives. We dug in our holes and waited and sure enough here they would come again and we would fight some more. It was hard to rest or sleep, it was cold, it was December. Pete and I shared a fox hole and you become very close at that time. At night we would take our boots off and put our feet in each other's arm pits so the body heat would keep our feet from freezing. We kept each other warm and alive. Sometimes it was so cold that in the morning the bolts on our guns would not work so we would have to pee on them to make them work. This went on for about one month you can only imagine what a group of men in the woods for a month looked and smelled like. We could not build fires; we lived on K-rations (which were not very good, but better than nothing). We were tired, cold, scared, and had watched many of our friends die. For about 30 days we did not move we just kept fighting and holding the area from the Germans. We did not know if we would ever get out of this, or if we would end up as so many of our comrades had. We thought about our homeland and our families. But we believed that America was strong and we were the best. We intended to win.

One day we were in the woods fighting and I came around a tree and there was a German soldier facing me. We both had guns pointed at each other and I killed him. It was the most unsettling thing I had ever had to do. You never think you could kill someone. He was just a young man like me, a new German officer. Neither of us wanted to be there but we were and it was either me or him, and I shot first. It was difficult to do, even in the midst of battle, and it bothered me a lot. I took his military passport and disarmed him. I am not sure why I took the passport; I think I just wanted to know his name. I think that is something that will always bother me. Killing someone is just not something you can forget or get over. I think because we were face to face it made it more personal; not like shooting into the woods and killing someone in the distance, although neither made you feel good.

Then one day the weather cleared, the fog lifted and we got our Air Force in. Our fighter planes came in. We were all so excited we all stood up and started yelling and cheering and they strafed us and we all got back down in our fox holes and learned never to do that again. So, from that point on we did not wave at them. They worked over the German tanks, the tanks were painted white so you could not see them but once one moved they knew where they were and they destroyed them with the rockets under the plane's wings. They cleaned out all the German tanks.

Towards the end of this month-long ordeal, a few good and funny things happened. One day towards the end of the 30 days we started moving and there was a chicken running in the woods and Pete and I caught the chicken and killed it. We could not cook it because it was not safe to light a fire so I hooked the chicken to my belt and I carried this dead, frozen chicken on my belt for two weeks until we came to this house in the woods with a wood stove in it. I will never forget the excitement we had with the thought of eating meat. We lit a fire and hung this frozen chicken down the tube on the stove and could not wait to eat this chicken. Then just as we could smell and taste this great meal, the

Figure 65. Paratrooper John G. Peterson demonstrates his marksmanship skills with the WWI era German Lugar he recovered during the Battle of the Bulge.

chicken fell off the stick and into the fire. Pete was so angry and just pushed me aside and tried to recover the chicken with no success. We never got to eat it. I think Pete was ready to let me experience "friendly fire". He could have killed me but of course he did not.

After our Air Force came in we were able to start moving further into Germany; and one night I had a great surprise. As I previously said cousin Ruey, Jr. and I grew up like brothers and spent our summers together in Middletown, Ohio. We had not seen each other since the war started. He was in the infantry and I had no idea where he was fighting in the war. One night in Bastogne area we were up in the top of a barn we had decided we did not want to dig a fox hole, and all of a sudden the trap door flew open and here was my cousin Ruey from the 79th infantry and he said, "Hey, Johnny what are you doing?" I was so excited. Ruey had heard a radio transmission that Kangaroo was in the area. Kangaroo was the code for the 101st. When Ruey heard that Kangaroo was in the area he got permission to seek out the 101st, to come and see me. It was great. After all I had been through it was nice to see family and know that we had both come out of this ok. The visit was short and the next morning we both had to leave with our group to continue our mission. We both made it through the war and remained close friends throughout our lives. My buddy, Ruey, died in 2007.

Figure 66. Members of the 101st Airborne in Austria. John G. Peterson is standing third from the right. Members of this company were to first to reach the "Eagle's Nest."

Another day as we moved, taking land from the Germans, we were close to a small town. We could hear German armor in this town called Huflar. So a recon patrol was sent out at night to investigate this. Pete and I were on this patrol. Before leaving on this type of patrol you had to take off anything that would rattle or make noise because you did not want to make any noise going into the town through the snow. When we got to the town it was surrounded with a wooden fence. We could still hear the German tanks in the town so we climbed over the wooden fence and snuck around two buildings and here was a whole string of German tiger tanks on the streets. We hunkered down trying to figure out what to do. Pete Pedersen had one bazooka shell and had the idea that we could do something to help, so Pete said let's see what we can do and he snuck around the end of the building and fired off the shell at the tread of one of the moving tanks. It was a direct hit and that huge tiger tank lost its tread and just started spinning circles in the middle of the road, Pete had disabled it. The disabled tank was right in the way of all the other tanks so none of the tanks could move forward. Needless to say we took off running with German soldiers in hot pursuit; they were shooting at us as we went back over the wooden fence and up the hill into the woods. That is when Sergeant Bill Green, one of our buddies, was hit and killed in action. I picked Bill up and was dragging him up the hill and that is when I got hit and took shrapnel in the leg, but they were still shooting at us so we kept moving. We got back to our foxhole and Snake Hogan our company medic looked at my legs and wrapped my legs and said I would be staying with them and to keep fighting. It was hard to walk but I did it because I was still ordered to be with my company. Due to Sergeant Bill Green's death, right there in the field, I was commissioned to Staff Sergeant Peterson by Lieutenant Tuck (right field commission). So, I took over the paperwork that Bill Green was assigned. I was making the onion skin maps of the battle field each day. We would mark the compass points so we would not get shot by our own artillery. Sometimes we did get hit with friendly fire though.

After that, in early February 1945, we were ordered to move and ended up near the Rhine River at a place they called Haguenau, France, which was a little town on the Rhine River and that was our holding position. The Germans were across the river and we would fire shots back and forth at the Germans. It was not long after that the 17th Airborne made an air drop. We were ordered to cross the Rhine River in rubber rafts and to keep moving and fight our way across to Berchtesgaden, into Austria. The Germans had surrendered and so the decision was made to send four of us up to Hitler's Eagles Nest. We went up there in a jeep with a gun on the back. The road up to the

Eagles Nest was a winding road and there were bunkers along the road on the way up, but everyone in the bunkers were already dead. If they had not been we might have been in big trouble. There was a dead German officer in the bunker. I took his hand gun. When we got up to the Eagles Nest it looked like a big white house, and we went inside to see if anyone was there. No one was alive there. When you walked into Hitler's Eagles Nest there were two large models of Berchtesgaden one in the summer and one in the winter. It was set up for strategic planning. There was a room full of Green Lucky Strike Cigarette Cartons from floor to ceiling and huge reels of American films. Hitler's girlfriend Eva Braun loved American movies. There was art work everywhere on the walls and tables. We secured the area and radioed intelligence that it was OK to come up to take over the area. We all took a few things, art memorabilia, from the Eagles Nest to take home. I carried out a marble carving of an archer and a carved Nordic hiker with antlers as legs. When the intelligence personnel came up to us, they took some of the things away from us, but not all of it. I was carrying the marble sculpture in my arms, but the Nordic skier was in the legs of my paratrooper pants and unnoticed by the authorities; I brought that "souvenir" home. There was also Hitler's train in Berchtesgaden and we got on this train and I brought home a knife, fork and spoon off of the dining car. Each piece was emblazoned with a swastika on the handle. I kept these items for many years before I sold or gave them away.

From there we were shipped down the road to Kaprun, Austria. This was like a resort village with a big lake. While there Pete and I were sent to ride a train to escort some displaced civilians to another town. On our way back, when we got into town we found out General Patton was in town. We got off the train and were walking in town but we were not in our dress uniforms; however, we still had our helmet liners on. We did not know General Patton was in town and we got stopped by the MP's and thrown in the brig. Patton came in the next morning and looked at us, growling at us and grumbled and then he saw the 101st Airborne on our uniform and he said all right you guys get out of my town and don't come back unless you are dressed right.

The 101st Airborne was stationed there for about one month. The scuttlebutt came down that duties in Japan were coming. They started issuing us live ammo and armor piercing shells. We knew that when you were given live ammo things were about to change. So here was the 101st and the 82nd and we were given the word that we were going to be on our way to the Aleutian Islands. They figured that we would fly to the Aleutian Islands and from there be able to jump on Japan. We were all in our Quonset huts talking about what we were going to be doing and then here comes my buddy Pete Petersen, drunk, down the road. He was waving the bottle around and yelling "They just dropped a big bomb on Japan and blew it all to hell." We said "ya right Pete" but he continued to claim that they had. We were making fun of him; we thought he was just drunk and making things up. It was true; we did drop an atomic bomb on Japan. So we did not have to go to Japan, the war ended, and we were shipped back to France. Once in France we were placed on the *Queen Mary* to be sent home. Then we had to stay in New York to participate in the victory parade before they would let us go home. This was a huge parade and everyone was yelling and cheering as we walked by.

I then went home to my wife Marylou and my daughter, Margret Ann. You just don't know how hard it is when you get home from war. You're scared and don't know what to do. You don't have a job. You have been gone for so long that you feel like you don't belong, that you are someplace you don't know. It takes awhile to get adjusted to home and every time a firecracker goes off or a car backfires you jump and you have flash backs of the war and although you remember the whole ordeal you cannot bring yourself to talk about it. I could not even share these thoughts and feelings with my wife. I spent many years not talking about the war and the things I experienced during that time. It took me over six months to get back to my home life. The experience I had in the war changed my life forever. You look at things in a different way.

I went to work at Buick and was given an apprenticeship to learn the wood pattern making trade. I worked for Buick for a few years and I then went out on my own to start my wood pattern shop in

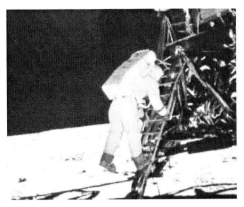

Figure 67. On July 20, 1969, Commander Neil Armstrong took his "One small step for man" on the Lunar Module ladder cast on a pattern built by John Peterson.

Saginaw, Michigan called Industrial Patterns. We did a lot of work for the Auto industry and for Batten Engines. I was contracted by Dow Corning to carve the pattern for the ladder on the space shuttle so man could walk on the moon for the first time. Dow used my carved wood pattern to cast the magnesium ladder that Neil Armstrong used to step down on to the moon to make his historic "one small step for man, one giant leap for mankind."

My wife Marylou died at a young age and I was left raising Debra Louise, a daughter of sixteen. My older daughter Margret Ann was married to Tim Lipman and was no longer living at home. I later married Kathleen Kelly Slade, our editor John Kelly's older sister. Kay had 4 children of her own; Sally, Barb, Sue, and Dick Slade.

Later in life when I retired from the pattern shop I became a wildlife wood carver and traveled around the United States and competed and sold my art work. I won the World Fish Carving Competition twice. I was a judge at the Ward World Carving Competition in Ocean City, Maryland. It was a very fun, enjoyable and rewarding time in my life. After my wife Kay died, I moved from Saginaw, Michigan, to Newaygo, Michigan. While in Newaygo I continued with my art work and the art shows. I taught my niece Nancy Kelly to carve and together we started Five Creeks Wildlife Art Gallery. I taught wood carving classes and judged wood carving entries at many competitions in the United States and Canada.

In July of 2009 artist Jason Heuser sought out a veteran, and after interviewing several choose me as the subject for his entry into the 2009 Grand Rapids, Michigan "Artprize Competition." He stated he choose me because of his World War II stories and his feeling that the two of us could make a connection as artists. Jason created a true to life pencil drawing of my likeness. I am very impressed by

Jason's hard work, eye for detail, and his artistic talent, this original drawing was presented to me for my keeping in December 2009. As a proud veteran I am honored to receive this work of art as a tribute to all of that served in WWII.

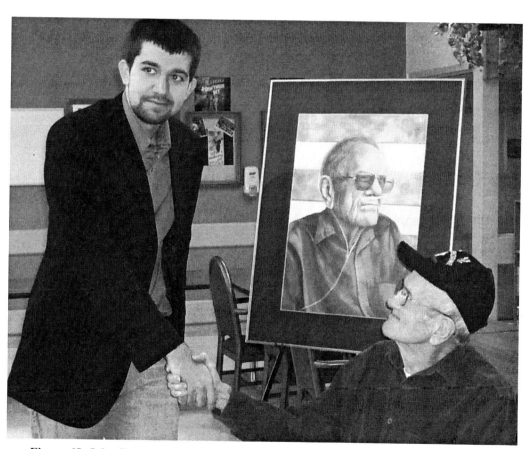

Figure 68. John Peterson congratulates artist Jason Heuser at the presentation of his portrait in July, 2009. Jason wanted to produce a veteran-themed portrait for an arts competitions held in Grand Rapids, Michigan. Photo provided by Christopher Kelly.

2009: ON DUTY IN NORMANDY, FRANCE
Evan Deemer
US Army, Operation Iraqi Freedom

My name is Evan Deemer and I am an American Soldier. I am 21 years old. I grew up in Lake Ann, Michigan, and went to Benzie Central High School. My parents are Barbara and Michael Clark Deemer. I am the grandson of Norma Deemer and a fourth cousin of Virginia Smith, both of who reside at the Village of Bay Ridge in Traverse City, Michigan. My father had Multiple Sclerosis and I helped take care of him as a young man. My dad passed away when I was just 14 years old. While my dad was gone and no longer able to teach me the ways of life, my experience while he was alive enabled me to grow up at an early age.

On August 3, 2005, I enlisted in the National Guard. I went to Basic Training and Military Police Training in 2006 at Fort Leonard Wood, Missouri. In 2007, was called to duty with the Michigan National Guard and went to Baghdad, Iraq, in support of Operation Iraqi Freedom. When

Figure 69. US Army MP, Evan Deemer.

deployed, I was as nervous as anyone would be, but I felt good for serving my country. My emotions included feeling scared, happy, angry, and amused. The responsibilities surrounding war really makes you discover yourself and find out who you are. I learned a lot about life during that deployment and it was during that time that I truly found the Lord.

I was deployed to FOB Rustamiyah south of Baghdad. Days included mortars coming in and blowing up in the area close to you and your friends, roadside bombs, and going out on missions and not knowing if you will make it back that day. Being so close to evil had me always asking for peace, guidance, and to make it back home safe with all of my friends. Just being so close to all of that made me believe in our Lord. A frequent way we described Iraq to those not there was to recommend that you turn your face to an oven that had been on broil for 20 minutes, have someone throw dishes on the floor to simulate the mortars landing around you, and pour a bucket of sand over your head to provide the ever-present grit, all the while surrounding yourself with your friends, making it all good. Due to my experiences in Iraq, coupled with the opportunities of the regular Army in today's economy, I enlisted in the US Army in September of 2008.

Today, I serve as a Military Policeman (MP) in Gafenwoehr, Germany. While serving as an MP, my days usually involve performing law enforcement duties. Recently, my duties have switched to training for combat, since we are scheduled to deploy to Afghanistan in the spring of 2010. Days are long, training is good, and I am making more friends.

Figure 70. Evan Deemers posing between two D-Day reenactors at the 65th Anniversary of the Normandy invasion.

In June of 2009, it was my honor to go to Normandy France for the 65th Anniversary of D-Day. I was part of a group of 20 personnel chosen to support the Secret Service in escorting the President as he visited Normandy. I was assigned to help make sure that all was good for the anniversary recognition at the Normandy American Cemetery and Memorial in

Normandy, France, overlooking Omaha Beach. During the ceremonies, I was only 20 meters from President Obama but I did not get to meet him personally. Fortunately, I did meet many of the veterans of WWII that were attending, and that was an incredible experience. I can't really describe what a really big experience that was for me. The veteran's were the best. I heard stories of their highlights of their military experience. I have so much respect for my military predecessors, the "Greatest Generation," and because of that day on June 4, 1944 we have the freedoms that we have today. The days at Normandy were filled with attending to our assigned duties but during some time off I wanted to say my own kind of thank you to all who rest in those grounds. I took some time to touch every headstone in the cemetery and to say thank you to the veterans who sacrificed their life for our freedoms and this great country. 9,387 stones are in the cemetery and I paid my respects to each and every one. I am thankful for what I have today and credit them because it is their bravery that kept America free.

Although I had a general interest in WWII throughout my years, this experience on the hallowed grounds of Normandy really taught me more than any book ever has. I learned so much more about the war, the invasion, the sacrifices, and the people who served. Why are those veterans called the Greatest Generation? It has to do with the patriotism and way of life that was valued in that era; an amazing America, where we

Figure 71. Evan Deemer standing next to a D-Day veteran and his wife while they attended the 65th anniversary of the invasion.

worked together as one and stood solidly behind our troops. That is what I love the most about that time frame, the era of WWII. My grandfather, Robert Allen Hall, was a WWII veteran and he passed in July of 2007 while I was in Iraq.

I enlisted in the military when I was just 17 years old. I enlisted so that our flag can be flown with pride and honor everyday all over our great nation and the world. For anyone who is interested in joining the military, know that you will be doing a job that less than one percent of the American population does. It is a big commitment but the rewards are endless. It should be no surprise that my favorite book is the Greatest Generation by Tom Brokaw. I follow in the footsteps of these incredible men, great role models and mentors for me, many whose story I have never heard yet I know that they sacrificed for my generation. I feel humbled by this opportunity to be a part of this book of stories written by members of the greatest generation. If anyone understands what today's troops are going through, it is the Veterans of War. I thank you for your service and I am proud to serve and to continue what you started…defending freedom and this great country …The United States of America.

I am proud to be an American. I am proud to be an American Soldier. Thank you for your support.
Your friend, Evan Deemer

Figure 72. Military Policeman SPC Evan Deemer on the beach at Normandy at sunset, following the 65th Commemoration of the D-Day Landings and Liberation, June 2009.

EPILOGUE
Norman Ainsworth Kline

There is an appropriate sense of ever increasing urgency to report the personal stories of our WWII Veterans. As this collection is published, WWII Veterans are dying at a rate of almost 1,000 per day. As an early reviewer of most of these submitted stories, I read most of the entries with great interest and humility. It should be true for all of us who can claim membership in the "Greatest Generation" that these stories make us very proud and humble; they surely do for me as one who lived through the Era of WWII.

There are many thousands of great stories about the wartime life on the home front and the battle front that have not been recorded, or ever talked about. We hope that this small effort will help to close some of those gaps and allow you to hear these stories from the authors, in their own words. It is valuable to hear these stories, as many of them began nearly 70 years ago and called for their authors to approach those memories again and share them here. Those days of global struggle are too important to be forgotten and we hope this publication will be helpful to many in the future. Thanks to all of those who served at home, served overseas, and those who kept the home-front going. I believe that each and every one of these stories could be the background for a very good movie.

Our specific thanks go to John E. Kelly. Without his persistence, determination, and patience in urging the contributors to present their remembrances, and his guiding their contributions into this collection, the job of recording and sharing these remembrances would not have been accomplished.

Table of Figures

Index

196

Figure 73. B-29s fly over the USS *Missouri* (BB-63) n Tokyo Bay following the 2 September 1945 Japanese surrender on the deck of the ship. Photo is from the Army Signal Corps Collection in the U.S. National Archives, in the public domain.